Cool Cats

Stories of Extraordinary Cat Dads

By Janet Vormittag

ISBN: 978-0-9986987-6-2

Cover design by Ryan Wallace (https://righan.com).

Cover photo is Marc Steensma with Dee Dee (page 89).

JLV Enterprises LLC
Cats and Dogs

Janetvormittag.com

Printed in Michigan, USA

*Dedicated to Norma Lewis
for her encouragement and inspiration.*

Also by Janet Vormittag

You Might be a Crazy Cat Lady if …

You Might be a Crazy Cat Lady if … (Vol.2)

Cat Women of West Michigan
The Secret World of Cat Rescue

The Save Five Series

Dog 281

More Than a Number

The Save Five Club

Contents

Introduction

The prevalent stereotype is that men prefer dogs while women favor cats. After all, dogs are man's best friend and women are crazy cat ladies.

In my world, men *tolerate* cats—they don't *love* cats. For almost 18 years, I've published *Cats and Dogs, a Magazine Devoted to Companion Animals* in West Michigan, and I've found that most people involved in cat rescue are women. There's been an occasional guy, but he's usually there because of a woman.

I have written three books about cats—two are collections of personal stories (*You Might be a Crazy Cat Lady if... (Vols. 1 and 2)* and the third one is about women involved in cat rescue (*Cat Women of West Michigan*). When I sell books at artisan fairs, pet expos and other special events, I am always super surprised to learn how many men love cats.

When the titles of my books are read, I often hear *What about men who like cats?* This usually comes from women, but occasionally a guy will tell me about his cats. One young boy even said, "What about me? I like cats."

Women have told me stories about how their fathers, husbands or boyfriends came to be cat dads. How they resisted it, but a certain cat or kitten worked its magic. Before they knew it, the guys were sneaking treats to Fluffy, making winter shelters for outside kitties or not able to move because a certain someone was snoozing comfortably on their lap.

When I announced on Facebook that I was looking for cat-loving guys to interview for this project, the response was overwhelming. In fact, an hour after I posted the announcement, I had to repost that I'd received enough stories, but I admit, a fair share of the responses were from women nominating a man in their life.

In my research, I've learned that many famous men have been cat guys: Andy Warhol, Mark Twain, Freddy Mercury, Isaac Newton, Nikola Tesla, Marlon Brando, Ernest Hemingway, Winston Churchill … the list goes on and on. And if you Google "Keanu Reeves and cats," be ready to be dazzled by some beautiful photographs— some a bit outlandish but nonetheless breathtaking. Yes, Keanu appears to be a cat-loving guy.

Have guys always loved cats?

Maybe they didn't dare admit it in a world full of macho, out-spoken, dog-loving men. Or perhaps they're finally taking the time to notice the intricacies of cats.

Women who favor cats aren't crazy; they're compassionate and wise. They know cats are delightful companions. Cats are loving, entertaining and helpful—who hasn't made a bed with the help of a cat?

And finally, it seems, men are catching on—or, at least, are now coming forward to admit their love of cats.

Tim Platschorre (top) hanging out with cats at Carol's Ferals where he volunteered for years. Tim (bottom) with Mickey who he found while at a friend's bonfire. He spent the evening tracking down meows coming from the woods and found a kitten. *(Top photograph courtesy of Tim Platschorre. Bottom photograph by Janet Vormittag.)*

Tim Platschorre

When Tim Platschorre and his wife bought a house in Cedar Springs five years ago, it came with an old red barn, two sheds and 16 outside cats.

"We were fine with it," Tim said.

Tim and his wife of eight years, Kathryn—sometimes called Kat or Kitty—came to the property to feed and water the cats before the sale was finalized. The previous owner had died, so they didn't know the names of their new feline family members.

"We made friends with all of them," Tim said. They also named each one.

There's Marie, whose nickname is Nuisance. She sneaks into cars if the windows are left open, and she has figured out how to get on the roof.

"We hear her walking around and say, 'It's Nuisance,'" Tim said. When they had a new metal roof put on the house, they worried Nuisance would slide off the slippery surface and hurt herself. Since they knew where she was making her ascent, they blocked it.

Dany is also a character. She likes to climb high into the rafters of the barn and meow for attention. "If I pretend to walk away, she comes down and chases after me," Tim said.

Several of the cats are gray with long hair—obviously related to one another. A neighbor had been helping the past owner get the cats spayed or neutered, but not all of them had been caught before he passed. Since most of the cats were feral, they needed to be live-trapped. When they took Stan to be neutered, they discovered he was a she. They didn't change the name, but now she is Stan the Woman.

One of the outbuildings was transformed into The Cat House. It has straw for the cats to burrow into when it's cold, a heated water dish, heat lamps and beams to sit on. They get fed daily.

There are only about a half dozen of the original cats left, but the number of outside residents is still high. Over the years, friends and family have brought feral cats to add to the colony.

Tim was no stranger to cats when he bought the old farmstead. "Cats were always my favorite animal," he said. People aren't surprised when they learn Tim likes cats, but they're often surprised by the number of cats he has.

A few years after graduating high school, Tim realized he wanted more in his life. "I needed to do something besides work," he explained. In 2006, he wrote a post on Facebook asking for suggestions on what to do with his free time. A girl he knew from high school suggested he volunteer at Jandy's Home, a nonprofit cat rescue.

"It was perfect. I got to spend time with cats," Tim said. He cleaned cages and rooms, fed cats and gave them attention.

In February 2007, 18 months after Hurricane Katrina hit the Gulf Coast in Louisiana, Tim volunteered for a week at Animal Rescue New Orleans. One of his jobs was to trap cats in an abandoned apartment complex. One day he set the traps, and then went sightseeing. He hadn't planned on being gone long, but time slipped away, and darkness had settled in by the time he returned. He quickly collected the traps with cats inside and was about to leave when he spotted a Humvee with armed National Guardsmen patrolling the area. The vehicle stopped and parked. The Guardsmen hadn't seen him or his car, so he stayed silent.

"I knew if they found me wandering around an abandoned apartment complex after dark, it would look pretty suspicious," he said. He quietly put the traps in his car, didn't turn on the headlights and got away without being seen. It's a memory he'll never forget.

Back in Michigan, he continued to volunteer at Jandy's Home. One of the cats he befriended was a long-term, skittish resident named Butterfly. Tim was still living with his parents, who already had cats, so he couldn't adopt her.

When Jandy's closed, arrangements were made for Butterfly to be released at a campground. A year later, when Tim bought his first home, Butterfly was re-captured so Tim could adopt her.

Tim found his next furry friend at a friend's home where he was invited to a bonfire. While enjoying the flames, he heard meows coming from the nearby woods.

"I spent most of the night trying to catch her. I was more focused on the cat than anything else," he recalled. He didn't give up until he had the gray and white youngster in his arms. He named her Mickey.

After Jandy's, Tim volunteered for Carol's Ferals, a nonprofit dedicated to ending the overpopulation of outside cats. He cleaned, helped transfer cats to cages, gave medications—whatever needed to be done. After volunteering for close to six years, he started dating Kathryn and life got busy.

Butterfly passed away a year ago. Mickey, now close to 16 years old, is the couple's only inside cat. Mickey disapproves of the outside cats. When she sees one, she tenses up and stares. Of course, it's Nuisance who jumps up onto the windowsill and peers into the house to torment her. Mickey greets her with a growl.

While Mickey is affectionate to Kathryn—she will snuggle with her on the couch—she is truly Tim's cat. Kathryn said as soon as Mickey hears Tim's truck pull into the driveway, the cat deserts her and runs to the door to greet him.

"I don't exist anymore," Kathryn noted.

Tim walks in, greets Mickey with *hello* and either picks her up for a hug or bends down to pet her. When Mickey was younger, she would bring a toy to Tim as part of his welcome home ritual.

Mickey has her quirks. She taught Tim and Kathryn that she prefers to drink her water, not from a bowl, but from the floor of the shower. When they notice she has disappeared, one will ask, "Did you water the cat today?" Meanwhile, Mickey is patiently waiting in the bathroom for someone to come and pour a glass of water onto the shower floor so she can quench her thirst.

Tim's job is delivering and installing headstones in cemeteries in Michigan, Indiana and Ohio. Traveling so much, he often sees roadkill. The one time he saw a dead cat, he stopped and moved it off the road. "I feel a close connection to cats and, for some reason, always feel more sympathy and respect for them."

Tim isn't sure what attracts him to cats. He does appreciate that they're calm, intelligent, independent and that they like to snuggle at times. He also finds it appealing that they can be loners, something he can relate to.

"They're good company," he added.

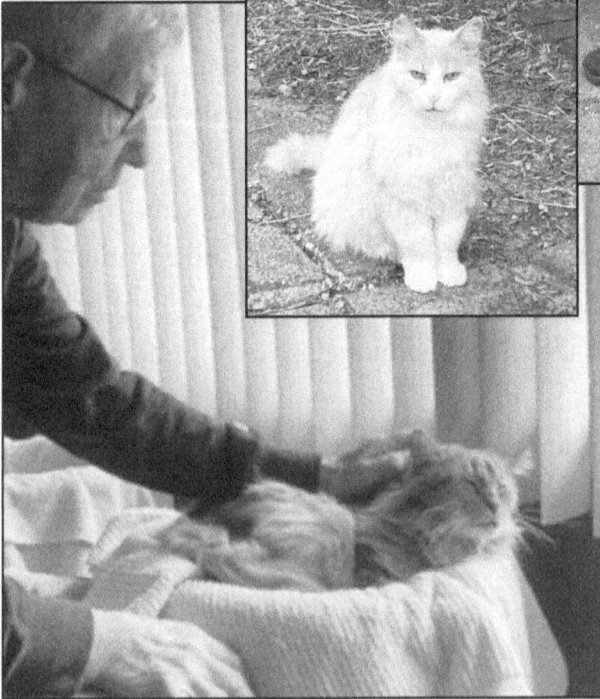

Fred Erbisch (top) showing the shelter he constructed for his outside cats. Boris (center) is the leader of the outdoor colony. Fred (bottom) giving Red, one of his inside cats a little loving. (*Photographs courtesy of Christina Lonski and Fred Erbisch.*)

Fred Erbisch

Having his bulldog euthanized was difficult for Fred Erbisch. "I told my wife, 'No more pets.'"

A year later, however, as the couple sat at the dining room table, Fred noticed a car pull in the driveway. Beth broke the news to him—while listening to the radio, she had heard a story of a cat scheduled to be euthanized unless a new home could be found. She came to the rescue, and the car in the driveway was someone delivering the lucky kitty.

Fred's reaction was one of surprise and concern. Beth had an allergy to cats, and he feared she was setting herself up for disappointment, but he was wrong.

"The cat never bothered her," he said.

The cat, whose name was Twerp, had been raised with a dog and acted like a dog. "He always met us at the door," Fred recalled. Fourteen years later, when it was time to have Twerp put down, Fred once again said, "No more pets."

But it wasn't to be. Within three months of losing Twerp, Beth surprised Fred again. While attending a conference in Dallas, Fred called home. During their conversation he heard Beth say, "Sam, don't do that."

"I asked if she had stopped at the humane society," Fred said.

He guessed right. Beth had adopted Sam—full name Samantha—shortly after she dropped her husband off at the airport for his trip to Texas.

Several years after adopting Sam, Beth died unexpectedly. Beth and Fred had been married 40 years. Her death left Fred and Sam alone in their sorrow.

"She had been Beth's buddy. She really didn't interact much with me for about two months after Beth's death," Fred recalled. He petted the distraught cat and left the radio playing while he was at work. In their grief, they became friends.

When Fred remarried, Sam was part of the deal. Fred and Pam have now been together 20 years, and Sam is long gone. It was Pam who first spotted a big, black cat scavenging for food in their backyard.

"He was hungry," Fred said.

The couple's home is adjacent to an East Lansing park that serves as refuge for deer, raccoons, skunks, fox and more. Fred and Pam always put out food for birds and other wildlife, and this was the first time they noticed a cat looking for something to eat. Fred put out a plate of kibble for the stray.

"The cat had bright eyes, so we called him Bright Eyes," Fred said. Bright Eyes accepted the food but refused to interact with Fred.

Fred was determined to befriend the stray. When the cat came to eat, Fred talked to him from a distance. "I would tell him how great he was," Fred said. Bright Eyes may have believed himself to be great, but apparently he didn't think the same of the guy doing the talking. When Fred tried to get close, the weary cat ran off.

Fred wasn't about to give up. Next step in the befriending process—Fred found a five-foot-long, flexible plastic rod, and while Bright Eyes ate, he used the end of the rod to gently rub the cat's back. Bright Eyes seemed to enjoy it. Over a period of months, Fred shortened the rod and continued the back rubbing. When Bright Eyes was close enough to touch, Fred made his first contact. After that, Bright Eyes allowed Fred to pet and scratch him.

"While we became buddies, he never allowed me to pick him up or hug him," Fred said. Bright Eyes trusted Fred enough to bring friends to share in the free food. First came a young, golden-colored kitten they named Marmalade. Then they noticed a cat living under a neighbor's porch.

They wondered if people were dropping off cats in the nearby park. Another possibility was that graduating students from nearby Michigan State University were leaving their cats behind in the park after graduation. The mystery was never solved.

Then came the kittens. "Bright Eyes fathered several litters of kittens," Fred said.

Fred started catching the cats and getting them fixed. "It wasn't cheap," he said. When the local humane society started offering low-cost spay/neuter surgeries, he took advantage of the program.

Over the past 20 years, Fred estimates that he and Pam have taken care of close to 50 cats. At one point, 11 cats were coming up to eat. Most were feral and only cared about the food.

"I have it down to a science. I put out wet and dry food two times a day. That's it," he said.

Currently, Fred is feeding four outside cats: Boris, Chuck, Missy and Buster. "Boris and Chuck expect to be petted. The other two just expect their food to be there," Fred explained.

The cats expect their first meal at 8 in the morning, daylight savings time. Fred tried to explain the time change to them, but they didn't understand, so he adjusted his schedule accordingly. At 8 p.m., when Fred's phone dings, he drops whatever he's doing to feed the outside gang their dinner.

Fred admits he talks to the cats. "They all know their names," he said. He gives them a daily weather report and apologizes if it's going to be cold, but he doesn't have much to be sorry for—he provides shelter for his outside buddies. The first was a doghouse-style shelter he built for Bright Eyes in the back of their property. He then built a larger, insulated hut with comfy beds. Neither hut nor bed saw much use.

Pam suggested they build a shelter closer to the house, so they bought two heavy-duty picnic tables and transformed them into a cat castle. Straw is used for bedding, and the tables are covered with tarps. Branches hold the tarps down and give the shelter a natural look.

When it rains or snows, the meals are placed inside the enclosure. "All our outside cats use it," Fred said.

The cats also have the option of going under the back porch, which provides more protection from the wind and cold. When Fred noticed the cats squeeze through a small opening to get under the porch, he made access easier and installed plastic tubs filled with straw.

Besides the outside gang, Fred and Pam have three inside cats: Sydney, Red and Streak. The three had been feral kittens and were adopted by the couple.

Fred, a botanist, spent 30 years at Michigan Technological University in Houghton, Michigan, first as professor of botanical science and then as director of the university's research office.

He retired from Michigan Tech in 1992 and moved downstate, where he was hired by Michigan State University to set up their intellectual property office. After ten years at MSU, he retired again and spent seven years traveling to at least 25 countries where he worked with scientists and government officials helping them learn how to handle intellectual properties. When he traveled, Pam cared for the indoor and outdoor cats.

Fred is also a wood carver and teaches the craft.

Fred never dreamed his retirement years would revolve around cats. He joked that Pam thinks he's crazy and has told him she didn't marry him to be the wife of a cat guy, but he has no regrets. He said cats are affectionate, rambunctious and funny.

"I enjoy them. They enjoy me."

Nick Luurtsema with one of his favorite barn cats, Nugget. (*Photograph by Janet Vormittag.*)

Nick Luurtsema

Nick Luurtsema had one outside cat for four years, but that changed when a stray showed up. "It exploded. It went from two cats to 30," he said. Nick was raised on a farm in Zeeland, Michigan, where cats were part of the landscape. "That's how I got my start as a cat guy," he explained.

In 2001, Nick's parents moved from the farm, where they had been renters, to Nick's grandparents' home a mile down the road. In an odd twist, Nick and his brother, Ross, continued to rent the farm. "I live in the house I was born and raised in. I never moved," Nick said.

Stray cats are an issue in the country. Some wander in from neighboring farms, but a few are abandoned. "Cats are dropped off. People see a big red barn and other cats …" Nick shook his head, not finishing the sentence. He doesn't understand the mentality of people who think it's appropriate to discard unwanted pets.

Nick found himself buying more than 30 pounds of dry cat food every week to feed the ever-growing number of cats in the barn. A neighbor suggested he call Scarlett's Cat Sanctuary for help. He made the call and explained his dilemma to Nicole McAndrew, the founder of the rescue.

Nicole offered to help with trap-neuter-return (TNR). She would live-trap the cats and have them spayed/neutered. Any friendly cats and kittens would be placed into the rescue's adoption program. Feral and semi-feral cats would be returned to the farm with Nick as their caretaker. Nick felt relief when Nicole was willing to help. "It was getting out of control," he admitted.

When Nicole set the live traps, she installed a camera nearby to monitor them. When a cat ventured in for a tasty snack and the trap door slid closed, she was notified via her phone and could come pick up the cat.

"She was here every night for about a month," Nick said. Nicole trapped 43 cats. "I appreciate the love she has for the cats. She's so dedicated."

Nick was willing to part with the kittens and a few of the adults. "If they can get a good home and not be outside, I want that for them," he said. He still had a hard time saying goodbye though.

When the trapping started, he hoped to keep 5 to 10 cats. He ended up with about a dozen—some feral and seldom seen. About half are friendly. "I have my favorites, and I didn't want to let them go," he said. "It would feel weird without them. Empty. Lonely."

One of his favorite cats is Nugget, a longhaired, orange tabby. Another favorite is Pig—a neighborhood kid gave the white and gray tabby the odd name. Nick isn't sure why that name was chosen, but it stuck.

The cats come and go as they please. They snooze in the sun and keep the barn and yard free of rodents. "I don't know what a mouse looks like anymore. My traps have cobwebs," Nick joked.

None of the cats come into the house, but they have comfy living arrangements in the barn. Part of the barn has been converted into a garage. It's heated in the winter, and there's a television, comfy chairs, and a feeding station and litter boxes for the friendly cats. The cats don't have free access to the garage—they're either in or out. In the winter they usually prefer to stay in.

Nick also has a feeding station outside. To his amazement, the cats share the food with possums. "They have their heads in the bowl at the same time," he said. The ferals take shelter in the barn, and Nick makes sure they have food and water.

Every evening after dinner, Nick goes to the garage to hang out—the cats wait for him. He watches television, has a beer or two and spends time with his furry friends. "I love their company," he said. Sometimes he works on restoring an old truck.

Nick worked in a factory for 16 years but now works in an auto body shop. He details cars on the side.

If Nugget is outside and misses the moment Nick enters the garage, he bumps his head against the door, demanding it be opened. If Nick is too slow in responding, Nugget jumps on the closed overhead door. His paws grasp the frame of the door's window and he hangs there, peering inside to get Nick's attention.

Sometimes Nick's buddies stop by in the evening for a beer. Not all of them are cat guys. "They ask why I like cats," he said. "I tell them cats have more personality than you give them credit for. That cats are good companions and fun to have around."

Nick also appreciates that cats are self-sufficient and curious. He enjoys watching their interactions and antics. For example, Nugget is sometimes found perched like an owl on top of one of the clothesline poles. Nick isn't sure why Nugget sits on the pole. Is the tabby hunting? Appreciating the view? It's a mystery Nick finds endearing.

"Cats are fascinating," he said.

Nick Luurtsema with Pig. This barn cat was named by a neighborhood kid. The odd name stuck. (*Photograph by Janet Vormittag.*)

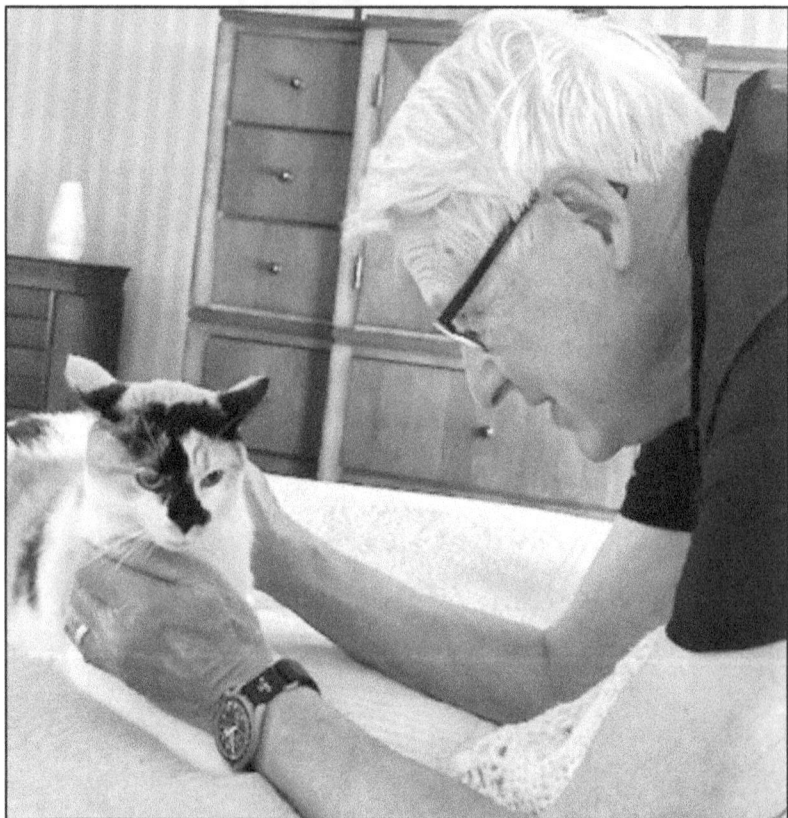

Flo was the first cat James Oliver and his wife fostered—they failed at fostering and adopted the timid kitty. *(Photograph courtesy of James Oliver.)*

James Oliver

James Oliver has childhood memories of his family's two outside cats: Patrick and Boots. Patrick was a gray tabby, and Boots was black and white. James has a photo from 1946 of himself as a two-year-old standing next to Patrick. He also has a photo that's close to 100 years old of his mother with a cat. "I heard my grandma liked cats too," he said.

While James has a fondness for cats, he also likes dogs. When he married, he and his wife, Kathleen, got a malamute named Mitsah. They have always been a one-pet-at-a-time family. After Mitsah passed, they got Frosty, a Samoyed. Then came Rocky, an Australian shepherd mix.

In late 2001, a neighbor contacted them when her dog found three kittens on her rural property. Where they interested in one?

"When Jett walked in the front door—it felt right," James said. Rocky had passed in 1999, and the couple had been without a furry companion for almost two years. The black kitten became their one and only.

"Suddenly people were saying, 'We thought you were dog people,'" James said. Understandable, since the

Olivers had only dogs for 30 years. "To everyone's astonishment, we became cat people." He doesn't understand the need to label folks as dog or cat people.

At the time, the couple lived in Middleville, a few miles south of Grand Rapids, Michigan. James and Kathleen were both teachers and spent their entire careers teaching at Hastings Public Schools.

Kathleen started volunteering for Carol's Ferals, a non-profit in Grand Rapids dedicated to reducing the number of outside cats through trap-neuter-return (TNR). The organization also had an adoption program for friendly strays and kittens born to ferals. One day, James tagged along with Kathleen to Carol's Ferals. He met Carol, the woman who founded and directed the rescue. He was so impressed with the operation, that he decided to volunteer. He helped clean cages and enjoyed socializing with the adoptable cats in the community room.

"It was an amazing operation," he said. "Carol is legend." Carol's Ferals closed in 2021.

When the Olivers retired, they moved to a condo in Kentwood. Their previous home had a fenced yard, so Jett could spend time in nature. Condo rules didn't allow pets to roam free. They knew Jett would miss the outdoors, so they installed wire-mesh fencing on their deck, where Jett could lounge in the sun and watch birds.

They also taught Jett to walk on a leash. Every morning, Kathleen took the black cat for a stroll, sometimes before daybreak. Mid-afternoon, James took him for a second outing to explore the yard and nearby woods. "He had a routine. He led the way," James said.

Jett lived 18 years. In his old age, he developed kidney disease. When the time was right, he was euthanized. "It was a tough decision. It was raw for a long time. They're family," James said.

James thought their days of having a pet were over. But they weren't.

In October of 2023, the couple decided to foster a cat for Rueben's Room Cat Rescue. That's when Flo came into their home. The scared cat spent the first week hiding in Kathleen's office. Flo was just beginning to feel comfortable in her new surroundings when someone was interested in adopting her.

"We had her such a short time. I bond quickly with animals. We were told we had first chance to adopt," James said.

The couple didn't think it was in Flo's best interest to traumatize her by making her move again. That's when they failed at fostering and made the calico a permanent part of their family. Adopting Flo brought a realization: "She could outlive us," James said—on his next birthday, he would be 80 years old. Arrangements have been made in case there comes a time when they can no longer care for Flo.

At the time of this interview, Flo had only been with the Olivers for a few months. The evening before, for the first time, Flo crawled under a blanket Kathleen had on her lap as she watched television. Two days earlier, Flo had jumped onto James's lap. "It took four months for that to happen," he said.

James feels Flo is insecure and wonders about her past. He noticed that the clanging of a fork scares her, and he questions why. There are no answers.

Flo is settling in and has already established a routine. "She's very predictable," James noted. Flo sleeps at the foot of their bed. In the morning, she waits on the steps to play laser light. James keeps the laser on a chest at the top of the stairs so he's ready for their game. When Flo tires of chasing the impossible-to-catch red dot, she goes to the bathroom and waits for him to turn on the faucet—she enjoys drinking running water.

"She's training us, for sure," James said. "I think Flo is the smartest animal we've had—smarter than our dogs."

James and Kathleen Oliver with Jett, the cat they adopted after being "dog people" for close to 30 years. (*Photograph courtesy of James Oliver.*)

James Oliver in 1946 with Patrick and Tiger, two of his family's cats. *(Photographs courtesy of James Oliver.)*

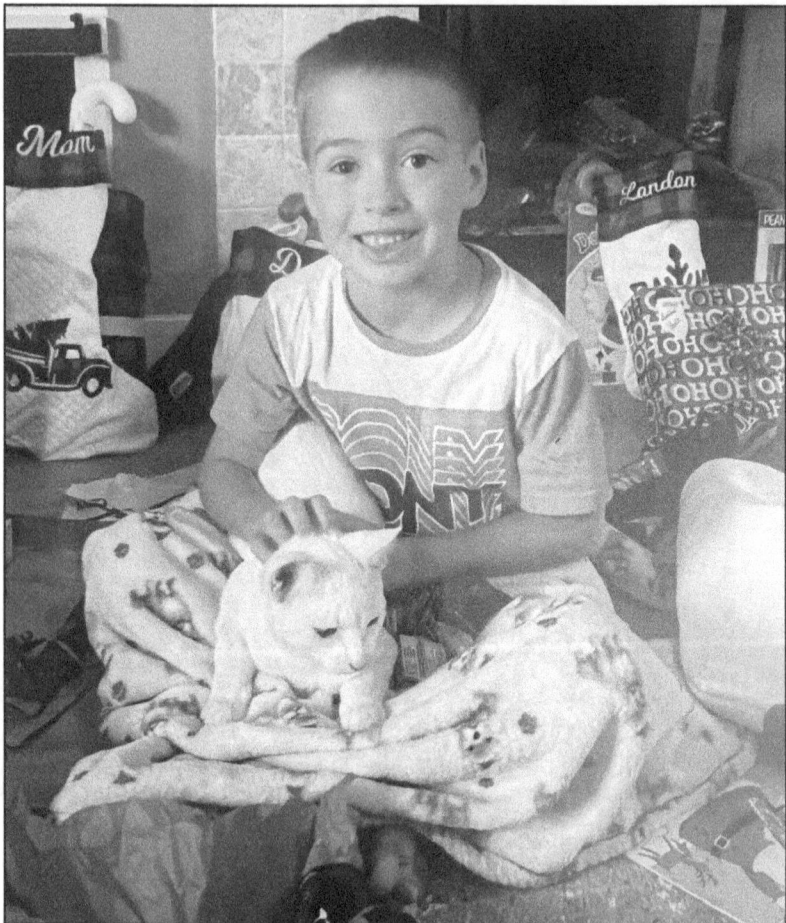

Brittin Dodge with Marshmallow. Brittin's mom surprised the second-grader with the white kitten. *(Photograph courtesy of Steff Dodge.)*

Brittin Dodge

Third grader Brittin Dodge loves cats. His favorite book is *Cats React to Science Facts,* which he has read several times. One of things he has learned from reading is that cats use 100 percent of their muscles when they jump. He thinks it's cool cats can jump so high.

When his mom, Steff Dodge, a real-estate agent, had a client with kittens, she decided to surprise her son. He was in second grade at the time.

She bought a cat carrier and other supplies, and when Brittin came home from school she told him she had something for him. That it was on his bed.

Brittin tried to guess what the surprise could be. Maybe a Pokemon bedspread? When he went into the bedroom, he was speechless. "He couldn't believe his eyes," Steff said.

When Brittin opened the carrier, a white streak bolted out, jumped to the floor and dashed under the bed. It took two days for the five-month-old kitten to work up the courage to explore the room.

Brittin and his mom did a Google search for names for a white kitten. Options included Casper, Snowball and

Snowflake, but the name Brittin liked best was Marshmallow. Often shortened to Marsh.

It took Brittin hours to get to sleep that first night—he kept playing with the kitten hiding under his bed. "He talked a lot," Brittin recalled.

The Dodges live in the country and already have dogs and outside cats. Marshmallow made friends with Dax, their Australian shepherd mix. The two often wrestled, with Marsh winning every battle. The pair could frequently be found cuddling together on the deck in the sun.

Marshmallow was allowed outside where he loved to explore. A year after being adopted, Marshmallow came back from one of his adventures with a wound that became infected. A trip to the veterinarian revealed Marshmallow had feline immunodeficiency virus. FIV is transmitted primarily through deep bites and compromises the immune system. The infection worsened. Even with medical care, Marshmallow didn't survive. When Steff broke the news to Brittin, he was devastated. "He balled his eyes out," she said.

Steff bought a casket at a local pet cemetery. Brittin gathered some things to put in the casket with Marshmallow—a white stuffed cat, a fuzzy bathmat, his favorite toys. They buried Marshmallow in their backyard under a tree next to TJ, a dog who had previously passed.

Since then, Steff and Brittin have gone through volunteer training at Harbor Humane Society in Ottawa County where they now volunteer once a week. As soon as they arrive, Brittin runs to the cat room to give attention to the cats and kittens waiting to be adopted. He also enjoys helping with laundry.

Brittin said he enjoys spending time with his mom, but said she seems to prefer dogs to cats. Something he can't relate to.

Steff said Brittin remembers the names of each cat and knows which ones he would like to bring home. "I'm sure we'll end up with one," she said.

Brittin has already decided his next cat will stay inside.

From reading *Cats React to Science Facts*, he's learned a lot of facts about cats, but the facts don't explain why he loves cats. Brittin thinks cats are hilarious, he loves to pet them, and he appreciates that they all have their own personalities.

"They don't actually have nine lives, but I really wish they did," he said.

Bill Bultema with his special buddy Oberon who was adopted through Crash's Landing. He was named after a pale wheat ale brewed by Bell's Brewery. *(Photograph courtesy of Bill Bultema.)*

Bill Bultema

Every cat lover has that one special cat. For Bill Bultema that cat was Oberon. "He was my Buddy. I say he was a human reincarnated," Bill said.

Bill adopted Oberon from Crash's Landing, a cat rescue in Grand Rapids, Michigan. Crash's founder and director, Jen Gillum, DVM, names all the cats she takes in. The white cat was named after a pale wheat ale brewed by Bell's Brewery in Kalamazoo.

One of Bill's favorite memories of Oberon is when they would sit in the backyard after dark. Bill enjoyed a cigar while Oberon chased fireflies.

According to Bill, he and Oberon had conversations. And if Bill sneezed, Oberon always blessed him with a gentle meow. Bill swears by it. If he faked a sneeze, Oberon would still bless him.

Oberon died in 2020. "It broke my heart," he said.

Bill's 42-year love affair with cats started in 1981. Recently divorced and living alone, Bill was at a pet shop looking for fish for his aquarium when something caught his eye.

"To my left in a crate, was the most beautiful pair of blue eyes staring at me," he said. Those eyes belonged to a male chocolate-point Siamese. Bill went home with fish but thought about those blue eyes all night. The next day, he returned to the store and paid the $20 adoption fee. He named the Siamese Maxwell but called him Max.

A year later, a female Siamese seal point named Tabu came to live with Bill and Max. Both cats lived well into their teens and passed within weeks of one another. Soon after, Bill's veterinarian asked if he would be interested in a five-year-old Siamese silver point whose owner wanted her euthanized. That's when Katie moved in.

A few years later, Bill's girlfriend, Christina, thought Katie needed a friend. So, Maud joined the family. Eventually Bill and Christina married, and their fur family grew.

Next came Thor, who had health problems. Then Chuck. Then Thomas, Ethan, Skeet, and Marshall, who was deaf, and his buddy Oberon, and the twins, Oreo and Cookie. At one point, the couple had nine indoor and one outdoor cat.

"I finally said *stop*, no more. Yeah, right! They are like potato chips: you can't have just one," Bill said.

In 2013, Christina was diagnosed with a terminal disease and given no more than five years to live. Despite the prognosis, she convinced Bill they should adopt another cat. In 2016, a stray found by a friend was added to the family.

They named the Russian blue Archer.

Christina passed away in 2019, leaving Bill alone with five cats. A year later, three of them died in rapid succession, including Oberon, due to old age.

"I was devastated when he left," Bill said. "There has been a lot of joy and laughter over the years, but every loss makes a hole in your heart that nothing can fill."

That left Bill with two cats: Cookie and Archer.

Bill missed Oberon so much he decided he wanted another white cat. An online search led him to one in a shelter in Hillsdale, Michigan. He made the 265-mile round trip and came home with one-year-old Tucker. He swears Tucker is the last cat he will adopt. With Tucker came the realization that the young cat could outlive him, and Bill doesn't like that idea.

So now Bill lives with three cats: Cookie, Archer and Tucker—they make living alone bearable. Bill is considering exploring the United States in a motorhome and hopes one of the cats will be a good traveler. Bill has three children and seven grandchildren and says they'll take care of the others.

Asked if his family and friends consider him a crazy cat guy, Bill said no, they consider him a cat expert.

What does Bill find appealing about cats? He likes that they're easy to care for. He also appreciates their independence. "They come to you in their own time, which is fine with me."

Bill loves the ways his cats curl up next to him and purr. He has no problem sharing his bed with them, but they do take up most of the space, leaving him a sliver of mattress to call his own. Cookie sleeps on the pillow. Archer prefers to be by Bill's feet, and Tucker is somewhere near Bill's shoulder.

He also finds cats entertaining. He enjoys watching Tucker stalk Cookie, and wrestle and chase each other. When he brings out a laser light, the cats go wild trying to catch the red dot.

Bill grew up in the country and always had hunting dogs. His first wife had dogs, and he liked them. He even bought a dog grooming business and named it Tabu, in memory of one of his cats. He has owned the grooming salon, along with a second location, for about ten years.

But cats have his heart.

Bill's cats are allowed on the dining room table—it provides the best view of the backyard with its bird feeders, squirrels and gardens. The cats also explore and enjoy the fresh air in the yard, as Bill is an avid flower and vegetable gardener. Most of the cats are content staying within the confines of the tall wooden fence that surrounds the yard. Tucker is only allowed out on a leash and harness, since he is an escape artist known to scale the fence.

Oberon escaped once and returned late at night, missing his collar and a tooth. Bill has no idea what Oberon encountered while catting around, but he knows it scared him, because Oberon never climbed over the fence again.

One of the bedrooms in Bill's ranch home is devoted to the cats, and it's where the litter boxes reside. But more importantly, it's a tribute to all the cats who have shared their lives with Bill and Christina. On the walls are framed photographs, with shelves holding urns containing the cremains of each beloved cat. Bill plans on being cremated, and all the cremains of his cats will be buried with him.

Oberon is the one cat missing from the memorial room. His photo and urn are on the top shelf of a glass curio cabinet in Bill's basement office. There's also an old, specialized license plate with OBIE on it.

In his retirement, Bill started a new business: Oberon Arms LLC—he is a licensed firearms dealer. Customers are warned there are cats in the house—so far none have minded. It's not uncommon for Tucker to oversee transactions from his bed atop a mini frig in a corner of the office.

"Everybody knows I love cats," Bill said.

Bill Bultema and Archer, one of the three cats he now shares his home with. (*Photograph by Janet Vormittag*)

Above: Doug Groening relaxing with Jasmine, one of the cats thought to be a medium who often played with a ghost cat. (*Photograph courtesy of Doug Groening.*)

Below: Barb's photo of Sam snoozing on her lap with an unexplained light next to him. She thought her finger had been in the way, so she took a second photo—it turned out the same. The orb was sitting on the arm of the chair. (*Photograph by Barb Groening.*)

Doug Groening

When Doug Groening's girlfriend, Barb, invited him to lunch, he asked what she was serving. The answer was peanut butter and jelly sandwiches. He was good with that—Doug was more interested in the girl than the food.

While Barb busied herself in the kitchen, Doug sat on the couch where a Siamese cat came up beside him. He tapped on his leg—an invitation to the cat to move onto his lap. The cat accepted and settled in. When Barb came into the room, she was stunned.

"He's not a lap cat," she said. Plus, Snoops always attacked the boys Barb brought home.

"The cat approved of me—and now we've been married 52 years," Doug said. Snoops was brought along when they moved into their first home.

In 1984, the couple moved into a house in Holland, Michigan. By then they had four children, and Snoops was long gone. They had adopted a black cat, Pixie, who was the perfect family cat. Their daughter, Anne, could dress Pixie up, including putting bracelets around her neck so that Pixie jingled as she walked through the house. Their son, Joshua, could get Pixie to do somersaults in midair.

Pixie had another talent.

"She was the first one to pick up the ghost," Barb said.

Pixie was a medium—she was in contact with the spirits of the dead, and they believe the spirit belonged to a former cat.

The Groening's house is more than a hundred years old, and the couple has been renovating it ever since they moved in. When the upstairs bathroom was under construction, Barb and her son, Peter, both heard a cat meowing upstairs. They knew Pixie was asleep in the downstairs family room.

"It wasn't her," Barb said.

It was then that Peter confessed he'd had an encounter with something in his bedroom while sitting on the bed.

"He felt something walk across the bed, and it startled him," Doug said. Peter didn't see anything; he only felt the pressure on the mattress of something walking. "He felt it jump into the wall where there used to be a window."

They concluded that the cat they heard meowing was what Peter had felt on the bed.

Another incident occurred when Barb and Pixie were in the hallway upstairs. Pixie began to growl at the door opening of the hallway closet. The black cat arched her back, and her tail fluffed.

"There was something in the closet," Barb said. Yet when she looked down into the closet, it was empty.

Doug also felt the phantom cat when he was in bed. "It pussy-footed us," he said. Doug sensed something walk across the bed and then felt pressure on his leg—invisible paws kneading his leg. "I said, 'glad you're having a good time'." He felt the cat walk to the edge of the bed and disappear.

When the couple heard about the Shadow Spirit Paranormal Investigators hosting an evening at the Felt Mansion in Saugatuck, they decided to go to learn more about spirits. The investigators had set up cameras in the mansion the day before and shared their findings. One photo showed faces looking in a window from outside, the only issue was that the window was on the second floor.

"After that I was spooked," Barb said.

"You wouldn't believe it if you didn't see it," Doug said of the photo.

When talking to one of the investigators, they learned female cats are more likely to be mediums than male cats.

The couple knows a toddler died in their house. The young girl's wake was held in the room that's now their bedroom. They don't know details of the death, nor the history of any cats living in the house.

They also learned spirits are more likely to come out when a house is being remodeled. Over the years, Barb and Doug have gutted their house—torn out walls down to the studs and rebuilt. Every room has been disassembled and revamped. Doug, a master electrician, rewired the house. They drywalled, put in new floors, moved window locations, put in new windows, had the plumbing updated and much more.

Pixie lived 22 years. After she passed, Doug and Barb were sitting on barstools in the kitchen when Barb felt something walk across her lap. It then walked across Doug's lap, and he felt it jump to the floor.

"We were startled," Doug said.

The couple adopted Jasmine, who they nicknamed Jazzy. Around the same time, their son rescued a male cat, Sam, and brought him home. Sam and Jazzy were the best of friends, but Jazzy also had an invisible playmate. Like Pixie, Jazzy seemed to be a medium.

"Jazzy could call it out," Barb said.

"And she would play with it," Doug added.

"She'd chase it like it was running along the ceiling," Barb said. "We couldn't see it, but she could."

At some point, the chase would end, usually with Jazzy stopping at a wall. The couple assumed the ghost cat went through the wall.

Sam never seemed to notice whatever it was that Jazzy played with.

Once when they were out-of-town, their son, Jonathan, called and said Jazzy was going crazy. They assured him she was okay and that she was probably just playing with the ghost cat.

Another phenomenon in the old house is the glimpse of dark-colored cat tails. Both Barb and Doug have seen them. Their 11-year-old granddaughter even saw one.

"It's strange. You're doing something. Your thoughts are somewhere else. Then you see it out of the corner of your eye. It just walks by," Doug said.

Jazzy never seemed to be scared of the entity like Pixie sometimes was.

Both Barb and Doug have photographed something they think is the entity. Doug, when he was out working on the couple's fifth-wheel trailer in the backyard. It was a sunny day when he saw something bright fly by. He had his phone and was able to get a photo. He called it an orb. This was authenticated by the Shadow Spirit Paranormal Investigators.

Barb's was by accident. She was sitting with Sam snoozing on her lap and decided to use her phone to take a photo of the sweet boy. When she looked at the photo, it had an odd white light on the side of it. She thought her finger had been in the way, so she took a second photo—it turned out the same. The orb was sitting on the arm of the chair.

Jazzy and Sam were best friends. "They loved to watch TV," Doug said. They especially liked shows about cats, bugs and birds. "They were our furry kids. We loved them dearly." Both Jazzy and Sam died in 2022. "We're not ready for another pet," Doug added.

Since Jazzy passed, they haven't had any more indications that the entity is around. Although they're still doing minor renovations, the biggest projects are done. "The entities are at peace, they must like what we're doing," Doug said.

Louis Goldsmith with Stancil who likes to be worn like a scarf.
(Photograph courtesy of Louis Goldsmith.)

Louis Goldsmith

Louis Goldsmith isn't shy about his love for cats. He wears cat T-shirts—some he bought, some gifted. One T-shirt from Fort Collins Cat Rescue is Barbie-Doll pink with bold black letters that read, *Real Men Love Cats*. He has cat-themed T-shirts for Christmas and Halloween and one that reads, *Cat Daddy*.

Louis feels that cats don't get the credit they deserve and shouldn't be compared to dogs—it's like comparing apples to oranges.

Louis grew up in an apartment in the borough of Manhattan in New York City. He begged for a dog or a cat, but the apartment was too small to accommodate such a pet. He filled the void with a goldfish, a bearded dragon and a snake.

His family often visited friends who had cats, which delighted Louis. "I would follow the cats around the house. I was obsessed," Louis recalls. He can't explain his fascination. "I just loved animals. I gravitate towards animals."

On a whim after college, Louis took off for Montana, where he volunteered with the Montana Conservation

Corps, an AmeriCorps grant-funded organization. He helped build and maintain trails on national forest lands. He found he enjoyed nature and the outdoors. Meanwhile, his sister, Jane, moved to Colorado. When Louis visited her, he fell in love with the natural beauty of Crested Butte and the community and decided to move to be near his only sibling.

Louis was hired at Fort Collins Cat Rescue, which later merged with Animal House Dog Rescue. The combined rescues became Animal Friends Alliance. Louis helped care for the animals, including working as a vet assistant. He became the foster care program coordinator and, later, pivoted to client services and worked as an adoption specialist.

"It was all hands-on training," he said.

In 2014, while visiting a friend in northern California, Louis finally got his first cat. The friend had found a stray with four kittens, and one of the babies fell asleep in Louis's lap.

"He chose me," Louis said. The eight-week-old tuxedo kitten accompanied Louis on the drive back to Colorado. He named his new buddy Stancil after a fictional character in a comedy movie. The name just seemed right.

"He's extremely bonded to me and vice versa," Louis said. "Cats are loyal, and I'm his person. He likes to be worn like a scarf."

Louis has taught Stancil several tricks. Stancil can squirm his way through a zigzag tunnel of cardboard boxes. Stancil knows the word *up*, and, on command, he'll leap from the floor to Louis's arms.

Stancil doesn't always wait for an invitation and sometimes makes the jump when Louis isn't expecting it. "It's a daily occurrence," Louis said. "All of a sudden I feel his claws digging into me, and I let out a loud yelp."

Stancil also knows his name and comes when called—unless he's distracted.

Louis has a formal portrait of Stancil that was made from a photograph he sent to Crown & Paw, an online creator of custom artwork. The process allowed Louis to select the outfit Stancil would wear in the portrait—a suit and tie seemed appropriate for the tuxedo cat.

Three years ago, Louis and his roommate, a woman named Andrea, celebrated their 40th birthdays together with a party on a houseboat on Lake Havasu in Arizona. Andrea invited Sarah, a friend from Michigan, to the gathering. The date was April 19, 2021—it's a date that changed the course of Louis's life. The attraction between Sarah and Louis was instant. A month after they met, Louis visited Sarah in her hometown of Muskegon. A month later he moved to the mitten state.

"I knew it was right," he said. He became a dad to Sarah's four-year-old daughter, Carmen, and a cat dad to her two cats: Miss Olive and Pickles. "The inn is full," Louis said. Three cats are enough.

Stancil was happy to have new feline friends, but Olive didn't appreciate the newcomer. "She stalked him day and night and hissed and growled until she finally got it out of her system," Louis said. It took time, but they get along swimmingly now.

The couple bought a house, and every room has cozy places for cats, such as cat trees with hammocks. A favorite napping place is Carmen's bed.

Louis is a pianist and keeps a blanket for Stancil on top of the piano. He isn't sure if Stancil likes to hear the music, likes the vibrations of the hammers hitting the strings or if he just wants to be near his person.

In Muskegon, Louis was hired by Big Lake Humane Society as its volunteer and foster coordinator. After a year, he left to help Sarah with her catering business. He also works part time at Big Lake Community Animal Clinic and volunteers once a month to take shelter animals to Village at the Oaks, a retirement community. Louis said rescue work is hard—there are cases of neglect, animal hoarding, injured animals, and the sheer number of cats in need is overwhelming.

"Keeping an upbeat attitude can be difficult at times," he said. "Compassion fatigue is real." He added that time spent working at shelters gives him a sense of purpose, and working part-time with animals is perfect.

He also found a part-time job at Muskegon State Park that feeds his love of nature.

Stancil is now ten years old. In Colorado, he was an inside/outside cat. Louis doesn't advocate for cats to be outside, but when he got Stancil, he didn't know any better. He's aware of the danger for cats from predators and cars. "I can't deprive him—he loves it," Louis said. It's a quality of life issue. Stancil doesn't go far and usually hangs out in the backyard and naps in the sun on the porch.

What does Louis like about cats? He likes their independence and intelligence. He appreciates that they can be fierce at times, yet have a maternal instinct that makes them overly affectionate

"I'll be a cat guy for life," he said.

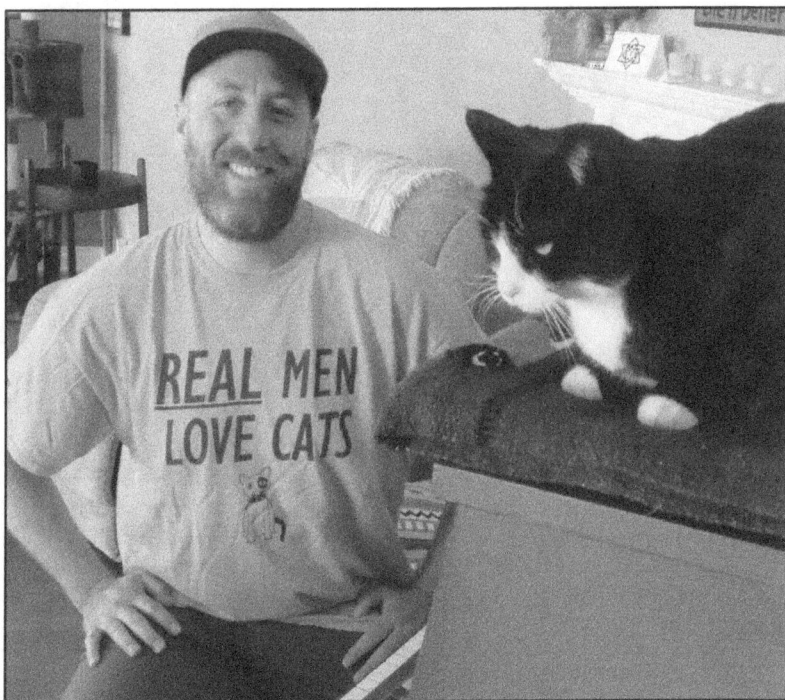

Louis Goldsmith has a collection of cat-themed T-shirts. Here he is at his piano with Stancil on his blanket where the music-loving cat prefers to be whenever Louis plays. *(Photograph by Janet Vormittag.)*

Gavin Hayes with Baby Bugs from the Looney Tunes Litter that Gavin helped foster. The family only partially failed at fostering—two of the kittens got adopted but Bugs and Wiley were kept by the Hayes family. *(Photograph courtesy of Miranda Hayes.)*

Gavin Hayes

Fifth grader Gavin Hayes loves cats. When his teacher's assignment to the class was to write a persuasive essay, he wrote one on why people should foster cats. The paper required three points to prove the argument and a conclusion. Gavin's points were:

1. Fostering saves lives, because animal shelters are usually full.

2. Fostering teaches responsibility—cats and kittens need food and water every day, and their litter box needs to be cleaned.

3. Cats and kittens do better in a home environment as opposed to a cage in a shelter.

His conclusion included a call to action; he told readers to consider fostering and gave them directions on where to get applications to foster for a local cat-rescue group.

The teacher gathered the students into small groups to read each other's essays. Afterwards, she asked if anyone wanted to share what they had learned. One of Gavin's friends raised his hand and said he now understood the importance of fostering cats.

Gavin said everyone knew they were talking about his paper. "Everyone in fifth grade knows I foster cats. They call me 'the crazy cat lady'," he said. It's a recognition he's proud of.

Gavin received a 1 on his paper, the highest score possible. He wrote his essay from experience. He and his family have fostered more than 20 cats for Scarlett's Cat Sanctuary in West Michigan.

Gavin finds cats to be cute, cuddly and comforting. He added that they can also be funny at times. Gavin explained that they failed at fostering once and adopted two cats who were supposed to be staying with them temporarily.

"It's hard to let go," Gavin concluded.

Gavin's family includes his mom, Miranda, and a sister and a brother. Their first cat was Kelcie, a 12-year-old orange tabby, who is now queen of the house. They found her on Facebook Marketplace and aren't sure what prompted them to take her in.

Their other six cats came from Scarlett's Cat Sanctuary. When Miranda saw a post on Facebook about a bonded pair of cats needing a home, they made the choice to adopt the pair—Joey and Archer. They were both a year old and though not biological brothers, they were best friends. Joey was high energy and Archer mellow.

Then along came Cheeto, an orange fluffy boy, who fit into the family dynamics.

Then they got a call regarding a young cat who needed an emergency placement. The tabby, Raisin, matched the energy level of Joey, so they adopted her as a playmate for the non-stop cat.

When Scarlett's needed a foster home for a litter of 14-week-old kittens, the Hayes family took them in. The litter, nicknamed the Looney Tunes, had cartoon character names. Two got adopted, but Bugs and Wiley didn't find a home.

"We bonded with them. There comes a time when you know they aren't leaving," Miranda said. The littermates were their only foster fails.

That brought the number of resident cats up to seven. Gavin noted that they all are fully armored—meaning they have claws.

Miranda said they're all family cats, but they each have a preferred human. Wiley is her baby and sometimes Gavin's. Raisin spends a lot of time with Gavin. Bugs has chosen her daughter, Dakota. Kelcie and Joey have chosen her oldest son, Ethan. Cheeto bounces between Gavin and Dakota. Archer will take anyone willing to pet him.

Educating his fellow students and fostering aren't the only things Gavin does to help cats. When Scarlett's Cat Sanctuary held an adoption day and bake sale, Gavin handed out flyers promoting the event to his classmates. He also made Shrinky Dinks pins of cat clipart to help raise money for the sanctuary.

He enjoys helping the sanctuary anyway he can. For Valentine's Day, fifth graders had the opportunity to invite someone to "Donuts and Valentines" at school. Gavin invited Nicole McAndrew, the founder of Scarlett's. The before-school party included donuts and juice, a tour of the classroom and a word-search puzzle. "It was fun," Gavin said.

His mom joked," He didn't bring his brother or sister. He didn't bring his mom. He brought his BFF Nicole."

In his free time, Gavin enjoys playing basketball. He's obsessed with dinosaurs and loves to watch the Jurassic Park movies and cartoons, which has inspired him to want to be a paleontologist when he grows up.

Besides seven cats, Gavin's family has four guinea pigs and a rabbit. Plus, at his dad's house there are five cats.

Gavin told the story of visiting a friend who didn't have any pets. There were no elephant-herd stomping of cats running up and down stairs, no meows, no guinea pig squeals, no cats playing or fighting.

"It was too quiet. For me seven cats is normal," he said.

Gavin Hayes with two of the kittens they adopted from the Looney Tunes Litter. Baby Bugs is on his back and Wiley is by his face. *(Photograph courtesy of Miranda Hayes.)*

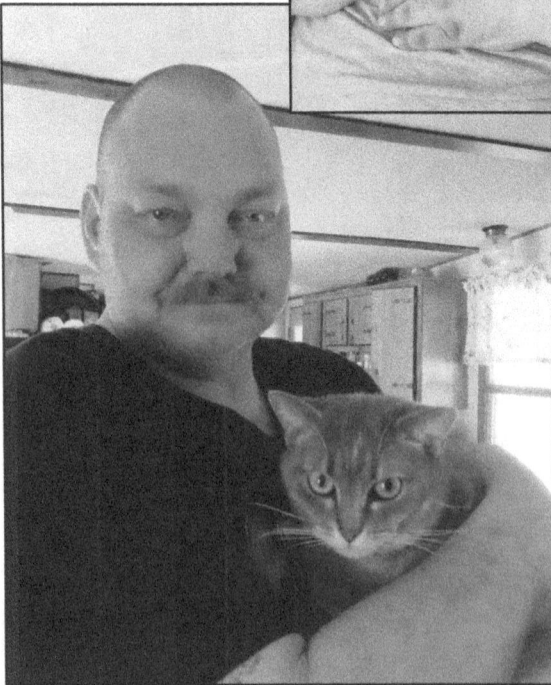

Jon Batema (top) relaxing with Kelpie, a kitten he live-trapped in a nearby swamp. Jon (bottom) and Hope. This gray kitty was found by Jon's wife and is the reason the couple got involved in cat rescue. *(Photographs courtesy of Tara Batema.)*

Jon Batema

Jon Batema grew up in a family with pets, but he never felt attached to any of them. "I didn't mind animals, they were just there," he recalled. None of the cats and dogs were fixed, so there were always plenty of puppies and kittens. That changed when Jon became an adult—he became a rescuer of cats. "They just find me. I don't purposely look for them," he said.

The first cat who needed him was Scruffy, an orange tabby residing at his aunt's house. Jon noticed huskies tormenting the cat, and he stepped in to protect her.

Garly found Jon at work. He named the stray after his place of employment, Gar Finishing.

Silky, abandoned at an apartment complex, found Jon when he visited friends.

Zippie found him while Jon fished at the Hamilton Dam.

"This man has rescued more cats than I have," Jon's wife, Tara, said.

"They just find me," Jon insisted.

Scruffy stayed with the Batemas and lived well into her teens. New homes were found for the others.

Jon is bewitched by cats' eyes. "They stare into your soul. They have such innocent eyes."

Tara has volunteered for area cat rescues for years. Her venture into rescue started when she found a small kitten at her mother's home. She brought the gray waif home and named her Hope. Jon claimed Hope as his cat.

Hope was an inside/outside cat, but then she disappeared. Tara and Jon searched for her and made flyers to distribute to neighbors. On day five, the wayward cat was spotted near her home. They suspect a neighbor's lost dog had chased Hope, causing her to go into hiding. After the dog had been found and contained, the smart cat made her way home.

After the scare of losing Hope, the couple decided her days of free-roaming were history. "She's an inside cat now. She can go into the enclosure," Jon said. The enclosure is an 8-by-34 foot fenced-in area that Jon constructed for their inside cats. It's adjacent to the house and is accessed through two windows.

"It's the best thing we ever did for our cats," Tara said.

"When it's nice out, they like their outside time," Jon said. Jon also built a shelter for two feral cats who live on their property.

Jon, an automobile mechanic, retired three years ago. Since then, he has joined his wife volunteering in cat rescue. His interests are trapping and transporting cats.

Jon likens trapping cats to fishing—if the bait doesn't work, try something new. In his experience, tuna and salmon work best—strong smells attract hungry cats.

Sometimes he does trap-neuter-return (TNR) where cats are trapped, spayed or neutered and then returned to where they were caught. The cats are also ear-tipped—the tip of one ear is surgically removed while the cat is under anesthesia. Ear-tipping is a universal sign that a cat has been spayed or neutered.

Jon sets the traps approximately a football field length away from his car. Then he sits inside the vehicle and waits. "You have to be patient," he said. Just like in fishing.

When Jon traps where there are several cats, he'll often catch one who has been caught before—the telltale ear tip gives it away. "It's catch-and-release. You wait for the big one," he explained.

When he catches the right cat, he feels the same satisfaction he gets catching a record-breaking fish. "It's a trophy."

So far, cats have been Jon's only catch. He's thankful a raccoon, possum or skunk has never ventured into his trap.

Jon and Tara's home is near a swamp where cats are sometimes dropped off. They witnessed someone toss two cats from a car, but they weren't able to get a license plate number. They caught the five-month-old littermates, and one of Tara's co-workers adopted the pair.

Tara works second shift at a gas station, and her drive home takes her through the swamp. She watches for cats and their glow-in-the-dark eyes. If she spots one, Jon goes trapping. They've caught five so far.

Jon said it's just not right that cats are abandoned. He wonders how house cats survive when dumped in places like the swamp. The answer is—some don't.

The last two cats trapped in the swamp, Grindy-Low and Kelpie, are still with the couple. Kelpie weighed one pound, nine ounces when he was caught. Tara said he should have weighed more than twice that. "He was starving to death."

Kelpie is now healthy and lovable, but it took four months before he was trusting and cuddly. "He's a sweetheart, but he's skittish," Tara said. She thinks his skittishness is a skill he learned to survive in the swamp.

Grindy is semi-feral and comes out of hiding occasionally, but he can't be touched.

Both are available for adoption, but Tara doubts if anyone will want them, since they aren't lovey-dovey lap cats.

Jon also volunteers to transport cats wherever they need to go. Most of the transports are provided for Kittens in the Mitten, a rescue devoted to the care and rehabilitation of stray cats and kittens, but a few are for family and friends.

Some cats need a ride to spay/neuter appointments. Others need to be taken to foster homes. In a three-day span the previous week, Jon drove cats from Allegan to Grand Rapids, from Kalamazoo to Holland and from Hamilton to Glenn.

"I like to drive. I get to meet people and cats," he said.

Besides transporting cats for a local rescue, Jon Batema also volunteers to live-trap stray and feral cats. *(Photograph by Janet Vormittag.)*

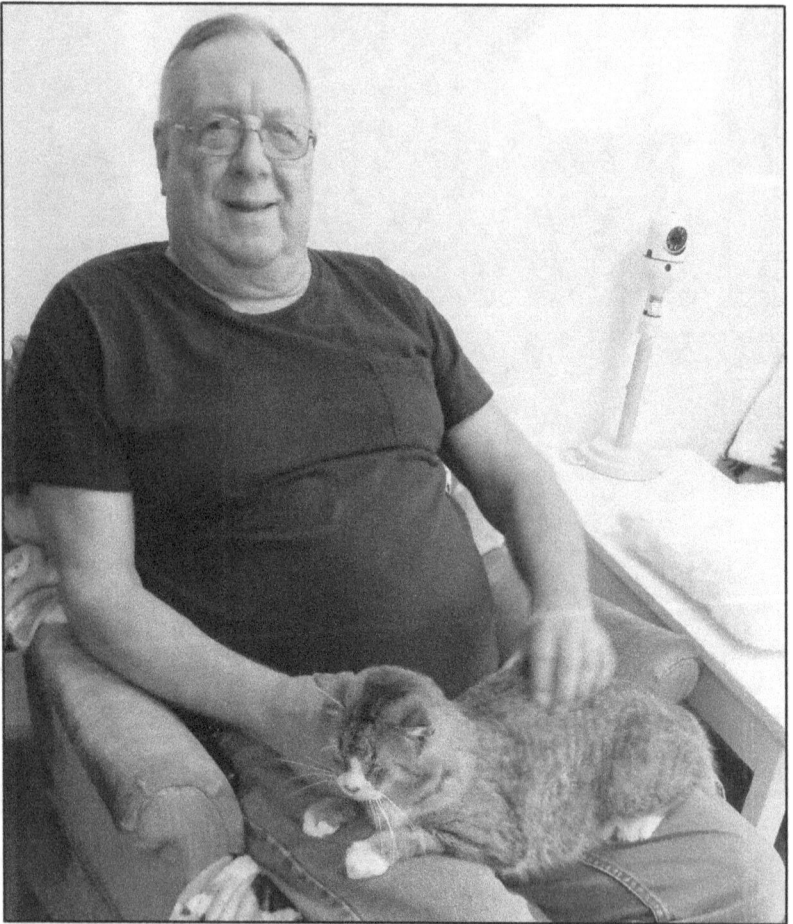

Jeff Stapp with Charlie relaxing on his lap. Charlie is one of the cats available for adoption at Second Chance Cats where Jeff volunteers. (*Photograph by Janet Vormittag*)

Jeff Stapp

When Jeff Stapp retired for the third time, he needed something to occupy his time. "I don't hunt or fish," he said. He joked that he already knew how to swear, so he didn't need to take up golf.

Jeff's first retirement was from the U.S. Army, where he served as a combat engineer. He next retired from a career as a construction electrician. His parents had run an adult-foster home, which inspired Jeff to return to school. Using his G.I. Bill benefits, Jeff earned a degree in social work from Ferris State University in Big Rapids, Michigan, and found a job counseling young kids and teenagers. He then transferred into maintenance while teaching basic construction skills to the youth. "It's easier to adjust a thermostat than it is an attitude," he said.

Jeff decided to offer his services to a no-kill animal rescue. When he looked for a place to volunteer, the closest rescue to his home was Carol's Ferals, a non-profit that specialized in trap-neuter-return (TNR) of outside cats. The group also ran an adoption program for trapped cats who were friendly and kittens young enough to be socialized.

"They asked how many days I could be there. I said three," he said.

For two years, three times a week, Jeff made the 30-minute drive from his home near Lincoln Lake, Michigan, to Carol's on the north side of Grand Rapids. The distance was similar to the drive he used to make to work, so it wasn't a big deal.

Jeff's primary task at Carol's was to socialize cats and get them ready for adoption. One of the cats who stands out in his memory is Gretchen, a 17-year-old declawed kitty who had lived with an elderly couple until they both died within a short period of each other. Their daughter brought Gretchen to Carol's.

"She wouldn't tolerate anyone," Jeff recalled. The traumatized Gretchen was given her own room where Jeff could befriend her. He sat with her, talked to her and reached out his hand in friendship. He was thankful Gretchen didn't have claws when she showed her displeasure by swatting him. After a month of Jeff's advances, Gretchen surprised him one day by climbing onto his lap. After that, everyone could pet her. "They called me the Gretchen Whisperer," Jeff said. The elderly cat eventually got adopted.

Another cat Jeff remembers is Dickens. The 22-year-old had lived with one woman his entire life, and when she died, Dickens ended up at Carol's. All Dickens wanted to do was sit on someone's lap.

"He was there until someone needed a lap cat," Jeff said.

When Carol's Ferals closed, some of the volunteers started Second Chance Cats of West Michigan. The non-profit gives animal-shelter cats at risk for euthanasia a second chance at finding a loving home. They also take in shelter cats with special needs. When they opened their facility, Jeff started volunteering.

"My job is to pet cats," he joked. He often gets on the floor, where it's hard for the scared cats to ignore him. Sometimes he reads out loud, so they get familiar with his voice. "It's fun. Once they get used to you, they don't hide. The big thing is patience."

Jeff is also Mr. Fix-it at the rescue. He has installed a sink in the utility room, repaired dripping faucets and assembled catios.

One of the cats in need of a second chance was a stray Jeff brought into the rescue. His neighbors had divorced and then moved, leaving behind three cats. One was killed in the road, another disappeared and the third abandoned cat found his way to Jeff's porch. He named him Yao, after the sound the desperate cat made.

Yao didn't appreciate being rescued. "He won't talk to me. I took him away from everything he knew," Jeff said of the cat, who hid under a chair while we talked. Other volunteers could pet the black cat. Yao would even sit on their laps, but he ignored Jeff. "I'm a little jealous, but I know he's better off."

Jeff said he misses the cats when they're adopted. "My wife says we can only have one. If it wasn't for her, I'd take them all home," he said, adding that he's tried to tell

Diana that two cats are better, but she hasn't changed her stance. Their one cat is Rubi, who they adopted from Second Chance Cats. They've had the gray tabby for three years.

The two cats before Rubi didn't have happy endings.

In April 2011, they rescued Snickers, a six-week-old kitten found in their neighborhood. The calico was diagnosed with a heart condition and died shortly after her fifth birthday. They weren't ready to adopt again, but then someone called about a kitten in need. That's when Boots, a tuxedo kitten, came to live with the couple. Unfortunately, Boots was diagnosed with feline leukemia. Even with medical care, she only lived eight months. They waited close to 18 months before adopting Rubi.

When people question Jeff about what he does, he tells them he spends three days a week at a cat house. They then ask what his wife thinks of his pastime. "I tell them she's glad for the respite. They can make what they want of that," he joked. He added that people aren't surprised he likes cats, but they are surprised cats like him.

For the past year, Jeff has been remodeling his home. The project limited his volunteer time to one day a week, but now the house is done, and Jeff is returning to three days a week. The rescue is only open to the public on one of the days he is there.

"Two days it's just me and the cats," Jeff said. "I don't have to share them."

Gretchen

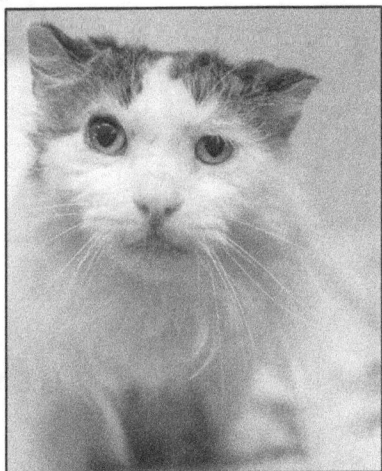

Dickens

Gretchen and Dickens are two of the memorable cats Jeff Stapp cared for while volunteering at Carol's Ferals. Gretchen was 17 years old when she was brought to the rescue after the elderly couple who cared for her died. Befriending her earned Jeff the title *Gretchen Whisperer*. Dickens was 22 years old when he was brought to the shelter after his owner died. New homes were found for both cats.*(Photographs by Karen Salyer.)*

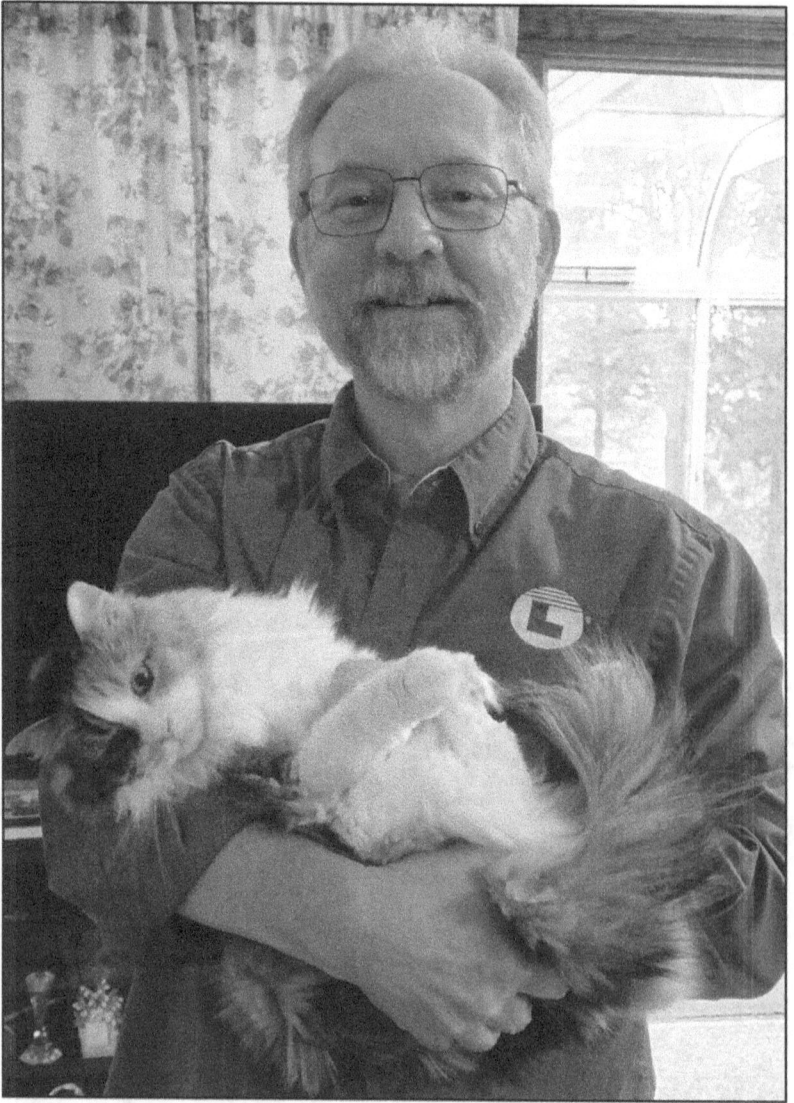

Randy Pearson with Betsy who was abandoned as a kitten and adopted by Randy and his wife. She's one of the three calicos the couple share their home with. *(Photograph courtesy of Randy Pearson.)*

Randy Pearson

By day, he's a numbers guy. By night, he works with words. But 24/7, Randy Pearson is a man who loves cats.

"I like how self-sufficient they are," he said. He also appreciates how easy cats are to care for—all that's needed is food, water and a clean litter box.

"I like low-maintenance because I'm low-maintenance," he claimed.

Randy loves how each cat has its own unique personality—a fact he was surprised to discover after he had lived with cats for a while. Some like laps, some are shy and some like to be picked up. He once had a cat who liked to play fetch.

Randy wasn't raised with pets. His parents rented and frequently moved. At one house, Randy recalled a fluffy orange cat standing on its back legs pawing at the sliding glass door. He thought to himself, *what would happen if I opened the door?* What happened? The cat walked in, sat down and made himself at home.

"Mom was not happy. She got a broom and ushered him outside," Randy recalled. They fed the orange tabby on the porch, but he disappeared after a couple of months.

The first thing Randy did after moving out on his own was to get a cat. The cat he chose belonged to two friends who wanted to get rid of "Kitty" because he peed everywhere except in the litter box. Randy thought the name Kitty was boring.

The cat's need for a new home was discussed at Randy's 21st birthday party, which he celebrated with a daiquiri party. He thought it fitting to rename his new furry roommate Daiquiri.

A new name and a different environment didn't instill in Daiquiri the need to use the litter box to do his business. A trip to the veterinarian revealed Daiquiri had crystals in his urinary tract. Perhaps the painful condition was the reason for his misguided urinating. Special food was prescribed, but that didn't stop Daiquiri from peeing wherever he pleased.

Once, when Randy pulled his canvas deck shoes from the closet, he wondered why they had curled toes. Then he noticed a smell and realized he had left the closet door open—Daiquiri had used the shoes to relieve himself.

The destruction of property wasn't a deterrent for Randy, though. "Early on, I realized it wasn't his fault," he said. "I had taken on the responsibility. He was my cat."

The vet prescribed what Randy called "downer pills" to relax Daiquiri, in the hopes he would take to using the litter box. Daiquiri was too smart to eat food if the pills were hidden inside. Randy had no choice but to force the pills down Daiquiri's throat. When there was only a single pill left, Randy held it in his palm while informing

Daiquiri it was the last one. To his astonishment, the cat plucked the pill from his hand and swallowed it. "He had a satisfied look on his face," Randy said. He feared Daiquiri was starting to like the effect of the downer pills, but since they weren't working, he was relieved he didn't need to worry about his cat becoming an addict.

Peeing outside the litter box had become Daiquiri's habit, a habit that couldn't be broken, resulting in him being confined to his own room. Daiquiri only lived two years after becoming Randy's roommate. After he died, Randy trashed the carpeting and padding in the room and painted the floor.

There were other cats in Randy's life, usually only one or two at a time. He was cat-less when he married his girlfriend, Wendy, who had three elderly cats. When the cats passed, the couple decided to adopt from a friend, who was a one-woman rescue, due to people dropping off cats and litters near her country home.

Randy and Wendy left the friend's place with two long-haired, calico kittens: Calliope and Cordelia.

Then Wendy got a job as a receptionist in a veterinarian's office. "She promised she wouldn't bring home any 'sad stories,' but along came Carmen," Randy said. Carmen's owner brought the cat in to be euthanized, but Wendy fell in love with her and offered to give the doomed cat a home.

Another time Wendy was driving home at night and spotted a kitten sitting in a mud puddle in the middle of the road. That's when Lydia came to live with them.

"I'm not going to say no to my wife," Randy said.

And then a friend found an abandoned kitten and convinced the couple to give it a home. That's when Betsy was added to the family. At that point, the couple had five cats. Sad to say, Carmen and Eden have since passed.

Randy thinks three is the perfect number of cats. If there's only one cat in a household, it gets lonely. If there are two, they play together and don't need a human. With three everyone is happy.

All three of Randy and Wendy's cats are calicos. "Calicos are the divas of the cat world," Randy noted, and the cats are treated accordingly.

Wendy has a rule that you can't move if a cat is on your lap. "Even if your glass is empty and your bladder is full," Randy joked.

They had to get a king size bed so there would be plenty of space if the divas choose to grace the couple with their presence at night.

Randy's day job is handling payroll for a charter school management company. He's also a writer. The name of his publishing company is EdcoCaly Press. The name is comprised of the first two letters of the names of the cats he had at the time: Eden, Cordelia, Calliope and Lydia. The company's logo is an outline of a cat with the company's name inside it.

Randy has self-published five action/adventure novels that include humor. "We need to laugh more. Everyone is way too serious," he said.

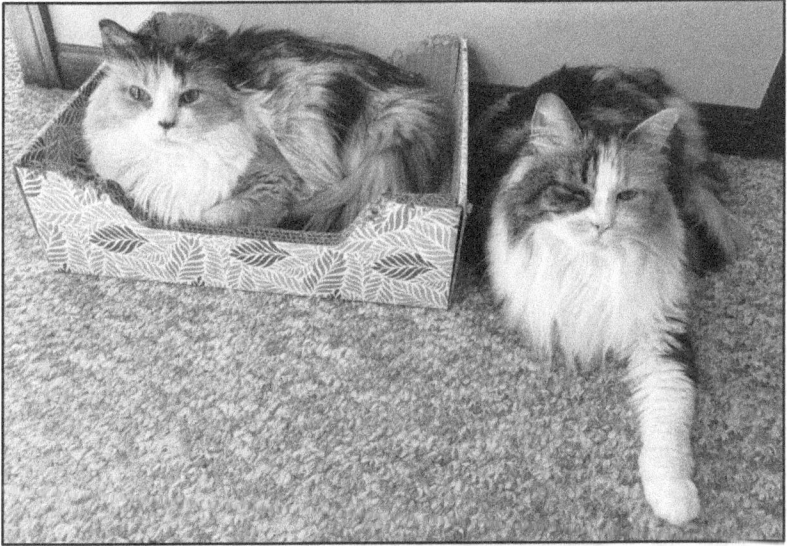

Above: Calliope and Cordelia, two of the diva calicos Randy and Wendy Pearson pamper.

Below: Randy Pearson selling his books that are published through his company, EdcoCaly Press, which has a cat for a logo. *(Photographs courtesy of Randy Pearson.)*

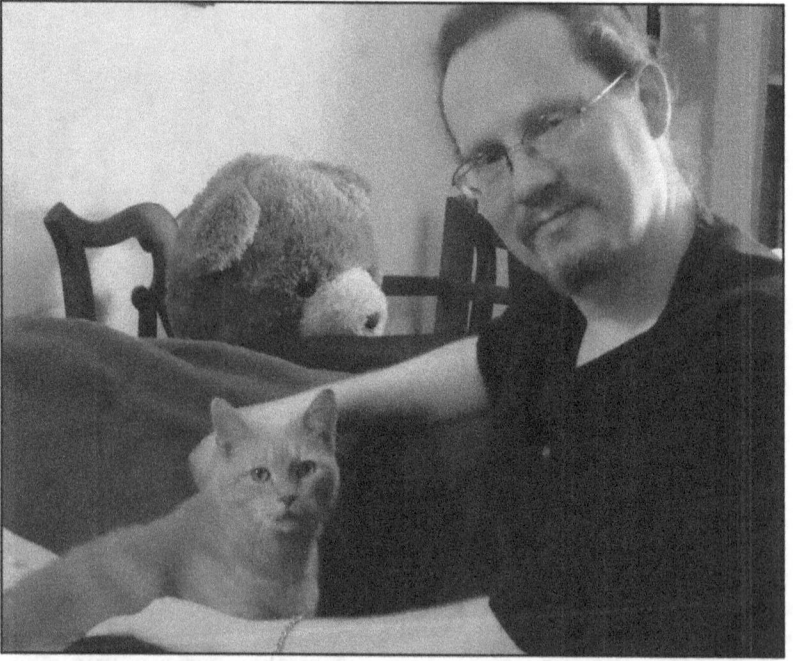

Ryan Wallace with Darwin, a buff colored polydactyl who is a sweet boy with rumbling purrs. Darwin's also a stress eater and struggles with his weight. *(Photograph by Janet Vormittag.)*

Ryan Wallace

Ryan Wallace, an artist who struggles with a variety of mental and physical health conditions, has three cats he considers essential to his support system. For him they function as both family and friends. "We take care of each other," he said. Ryan refers to his furry family of three as the Kidokas or Kidoka Clan. The term started out as simply referring to the cats as kiddos and evolved from there. He thinks of it like the term Jellicle for the felines in Andrew Webbers famous play *Cats*.

Ryan knows his cats' personalities, quirks and medical issues. "I don't seem to get cats that are easy," Ryan said, but he believes that when you take in a cat, you make a commitment, no matter what. "Just because it's an inconvenience doesn't mean you get rid of them."

Let's meet the current Kidoka Clan. First up are four-year-old littermates Tesla and Darwin. Ryan prefers to get two kittens at a time so the newcomers have same-age playmates.

Tesla, an orange tiger, is high energy and a bit crazy like the scientist he's named after. Nikola Tesla, a physicist and inventor, attributed his interest in electricity to his cat,

Macak. On a cold, dry winter night, Nikola had an *aha* moment when static electricity sparked as he stroked Macak's furry coat.

Tesla the cat has a variety of anxiety issues and prefers to be under the couch when strangers, such as the furnace repair man, are in his space. Normally, he is loving and needy, not liking to be separated from Ryan for even a few hours

His medical condition is cystitis, a type of lower urinary tract disease that causes inflammation of the urethra. The cause is unknown, but experts believe stress plays a role. Tesla is on a special diet, and Ryan does his best to keep stress levels low. A challenging task with Tesla's neediness and anxiety issues. It has also imposed some limits on Ryan's social life. Still, Ryan considers Tesla his best friend, and the orange tiger is always there for him as he struggles with his own anxiety issues.

Tesla's brother Darwin, a buff colored polydactyl, is a sweet boy with rumbling purrs.

"He struggles with his weight. He's a stress eater," Ryan explained as he introduced the big boy sitting on a cat tree overlooking a backyard pond.

One of the stresses in Darwin's life is having his nails trimmed. He is violently opposed to the procedure—he fights it like he is being murdered. But trimming Darwin's claws isn't optional. For some reason, his claws will constantly overgrow into his skin if not trimmed. When the ordeal is finished, Darwin runs to the food bowl and munches away his stress.

Ryan buys him toys, hoping Darwin will play away those extra calories. One such toy is a feather on a spring wire. Darwin swats and chases the feather in hopes of catching and killing his prey, oblivious to the real motive for the play.

The third Kidoka is Hermes, a 14-year-old Maine coon. "Hermes is the lover of the family. He teaches all the other kitties how to snuggle," Ryan said.

Ryan's morning ritual includes sitting cross-legged on the couch with Hermes. "He lays on his back with his head in my lap and just looks up at me. That look is love. I pet him and tell him he's beautiful and that I love him."

Ryan had dogs and cats as a kid but didn't start his love affair with felines until he married and became dad to Baby, a gray and white short-haired kitty. "That cat loved me to death and changed how I felt about cats. I've been a cat person ever since," he said.

Ryan's marriage didn't last, but his fondness for cats did. He spoke with affection of the cats he and his wife, Ang, shared during their marriage. Punk and Pooka were mere kittens when they walked up to Ang while she was camping. She brought them home with a question, "Can we keep them?"

Of course, the answer was yes. The long-haired tuxedo babies fit in the palm of Ryan's hand and became a wonderful addition to the family. Nicknamed the Twin Ps, the siblings had a love-fight relationship. Punk was a bruiser, a bully, a masochist and had scars on his nose to prove it. His favorite activity was harassing his sister. He would pick on Pooka until she pulled out her claws to tell him to back off. "He always started it. She always finished it, but he seemed to like it," Ryan said. Ironically, Pooka never had wounds or scars on her face.

Punk developed an issue of bleeding from his nose. Tests were inconclusive, but cancer was a suspect. He was given six months to live. "We were devastated. Punk and Pooka were like our biological children," Ryan said. But six months came and went, and Punk was still alive. Whenever he got an infection, such as a cold or urinary tract infection, the bleeding returned. He would get antibiotics and medication to clot his blood. Three years later, when Punk was nine, the couple woke to find Punk had passed in the night. They buried him in their backyard.

A couple of years later, they discovered Pooka had a mass behind one of her eyes. They opted for surgery to remove the mass and the eye, but only a month later the mass returned, this time inside her mouth. The difficult decision was made to have her euthanized. Pooka died three years and three days after her brother passed.

When Ang wanted a Maine coon, they found a breeder with a litter of kittens. Ang had a hard time deciding which of two kittens she wanted, so the breeder made them a deal: buy one, get half off the other one. That's when littermates Hermes and Ares joined the family.

Ares died in 2016 from a saddle thrombus, a blood clot that blocks blood supply to the back legs. Ares was a quiet cat who never meowed. When he started screaming and couldn't move his back legs, they knew something was wrong. There was no treatment. Ares was only six years old.

Ryan was reflective of the short time Ares lived. "Better to have Ares for the time we had him than not to have Ares at all," he said.

When a neighbor needed to get rid of a kitten, Ang brought the little one home in a cardboard box. "He jumped out like a Jack-in-a-box," Ryan recalled. While trying to think of a name, they called him Munchkin and then Munchichi. After the kitten started responding to Munchichi, they knew they'd found his name. Eventually it became shortened to Chi-chi.

"He was a problem child," Ryan said.

The orange and white kitten had anxiety and was always in trouble. His most memorable accomplishment was destroying all the blinds in the house—all 20 of them. He loved the curtains that replaced the demolished blinds. "He put teeth holes in each one, and when closed, they looked like starlight," Ryan said.

All the mischief endeared the cats to Ryan.

"They get into trouble and don't listen. It's like having permanent toddlers, and I like that about them," he said.

Chi-chi's saga included an escape from the couple's Wyoming home. A week after he disappeared, he was found in downtown Grand Rapids. How he traveled so far remains a mystery, but when he was returned, he wasn't feeling well. He was hospitalized and given palliative care and fluids. The veterinarian didn't think he would survive, but he did.

A few years later, Chi-chi screamed in pain and was rushed to the vet. It was suspected he ingested one of Ryan's meds—Ryan has cystic fibrosis and takes a lot of medications. But after listing all the drugs, meds were ruled out. Just when they thought Chi-chi had stabilized, he had a seizure. The couple was asked permission to cease life-saving care, and they gave it.

When the couple divorced, Tesla's attachment issues ensured he would go with Ryan. Ang didn't want to separate the cats, so she let Ryan keep them all. "Mama misses you, baby," Ryan whispered to Hermes as he talked about Ang's decision to have him keep the cats.

Why is Ryan so attracted to cats?

"I love cats for a lot of reasons. They're cute—I'm a big fan of cute. I like that they act tougher than they are, that they are mischievous and silly. I love their rumbly purrs, their little comments and demands. Their beauty and grace. I love how needy and sweet they can be. Cats are the closest I'm getting to having kids."

Ryan Wallace with Hermes, a 14-year-old Maine Coon who is the lover of the family. *(Photograph by Janet Vormittag.)*

Marc Steensma with three-legged Yardley who was adopted from Crash's Landing where Marc volunteered. (*Photograph courtesy of Marc Steensma.*)

Marc Steensma

When Marc Steensma was young, he was called a cat whisperer, and he hated it. "I'm a guy. 'Cat wrangler' would have been better," he said. Now he's not bothered by the title.

"There's nothing like a cat cuddling with you. It's enriching," he said. "They want to put their smell all over you so everyone knows you're theirs."

Marc's affinity for cats started as a teenager. As a kid, he spent weekends with his dad, but that came to a tragic halt after his father died when Marc was 14

"It left a void. I started volunteering for Crash's Landing, and that helped me process the trauma," Marc explained. Crash's Landing, based in West Michigan, is a no-kill, free-roam rescue and placement center for at-risk cats.

Marc's first role at the rescue was cuddling cats and giving them attention. From there, he graduated to litter box scooper and cleaner. In time, he advanced to administering health checks and medicating cats. He became known for befriending the scared and shy ones, which is when he earned the label of cat whisperer.

Marc believes that when you love a cat in a rescue environment, that love is transmitted to the cat's new owner. "You can teach them how to love," he said.

Marc eventually took on the task of training new volunteers. He also photographed the cats for the group's website and created videos. He helped with fundraising and recalled an event that raised close to $50,000. He was thrilled and amazed to be part of such a successful campaign.

While volunteering for Crash's, Marc desperately wanted to bring a cat home, but his mother always said no. Instead of continually pleading, he tried a different tactic. He had Mr. Bones, the cat he wanted to adopt, write a letter to his mom. The eight-month-old black kitten wrote that he was having a hard time adjusting to life at the rescue, and he just wanted stability and love. Marc wrote it in scribbly handwriting and signed it with a paw print.

"I didn't stop until she said yes," Marc said. It took two letters over the course of a week for his mom to agree to meet the needy cat. The visit to Mr. Bones cinched the deal. Mr. Bones wasn't the only kitty Marc adopted. "The floodgates were opened," he recalled.

Next came Spike, Millie, Conner, Franklin and ZZ Top, a tuxedo cat who was a *sharply dressed man*. Then came three-legged Yardley (Get it? There's three feet in a yard).

Marc credits Dr. Jen Gillum, founder and director of Crash's Landing, for the clever names. She has a reputation for creatively naming the cats admitted into the rescue.

Most of the cats Marc adopted were either black or black and white. "They're the ones overlooked. I felt compassion for them," he said. He chuckled when he remembered how neighborhood kids didn't come around his house at Halloween.

Dark colored cats are drawn to Marc. "They light up when I walk into the room. They stare at me. It's wild," he said. He doesn't have an explanation, other than maybe they can sense the special place they hold in his heart.

"All the animals we have loved live on in our hearts," he said.

Marc volunteered at Crash's Landing for ten years. After college, he had to leave his cats with his mom when he got a job with the Department of Defense. His work as a military facilities planner took him to California, Hawaii, Virginia and Japan.

When he had enough of government work, he took a one-year ministry job on the south side of Chicago. Then the perfect opportunity came his way. "It was one of those God doors—it came full circle," he said.

While Marc was absent from West Michigan, his cousin, Jen Kuyt, started the Country Cat Lady, a non-profit sanctuary for cats that specializes in therapy cats. She and her mother (Marc's aunt), Vicki Steensma, already co-owned The Catz Den. Jen's dream of having a multi-purpose facility in Wayland was coming true, and she needed help.

So, Marc was hired as the building manager of The Catz Den, a rental space for events like birthday parties, showers, anniversaries—any celebratory occasion. The rental fees support the mission of the Country Cat Lady. The building also has an adoption center with therapy cats and cats available for adoption. The therapy cats are taken to area nursing homes for visits. The Den also has a small gift shop, couches, tables, comfy chairs, a TV nook, sound system and more. Plans for the space are still evolving.

Marc's workday starts by going to Jen's house, where the Country Cat Lady has its main campus. There he has morning chores for about 25 cats and kittens. Some of the kittens come from trap-neuter-return situations and require socialization. Marc works his charm and helps prepare them for adoption.

He then travels to The Catz Den and looks in on the cats in the adoption room. "I check their water and food and that everyone is accounted for," he said. Volunteers take care of the cats, but he is responsible for overseeing their care and is the backup if a volunteer is a no-show.

Marc feels it's important to know every cat's name and to use it when talking to them. "It's the affection, the tone in your voice," he explained.

Part of his work includes writing the social media posts for the adoptable cats. The posts include photos—and sometimes a video—and details of the cat's personality. For example:

Mouse is an ultra-adorable, very gentle, super loving kitty that will bring a big wave of calm with her. She is extremely sweet, and we can't quite tag her with the "shy" label because she isn't. She's just calm, reserved, gentle and sweet. She loves her ear rubs and affection.

The post included three photos of the gray and white tiger kitty. Mouse found her new home within a couple of days.

Marc does have a dog, Koti. He claims the border collie thinks of herself as a cat, since she had been raised with 13 cats in a hoarding situation. Marc's aunt fostered Koti, but the dog clung to Marc whenever he was around. Koti had a meet-and-greet with a potential adopter, but they were a no-show. She was meant to be with Marc.

"She adopted me," Marc claimed.

Marc recently bought a house in Allegan and is starting to fill it with pets. Besides Koti, he already has two cats. He's a cat dad to Jozie, a 12-year-old Russian Blue who belongs to his girlfriend. Then there's nine-month-old Atlas—the fluffy white Persian-mix was brought to The Catz Den after his kitty parent was given a terminal cancer diagnosis. Marc could tell the young cat had personality under his shy demeanor.

"He wasn't going to break out of that shell at The Catz Den," he said. Marc adopted the youngster.

When Marc stepped into his role at The Catz Den, he said the 14-year-old version of himself became activated, that—taking care of cats is second nature. He's sure that working with animals is what he's meant to be doing.

"This fell right into my calling," he said.

Mike Behrens being greeted by Otis as he brings food into one of the cat rooms at Second Chance Cats of West Michigan where he volunteers. *(Photograph by Janet Vormittag.)*

Mike Behrens

When Mike Behrens needed a new license plate for his car, he decided to have some fun and requested it be personalized. His new plate, CAT D4D, reveals to people driving behind him how he feels about his all-time favorite pet.

"I just love cats. Everybody who knows me knows I like cats. Somehow, I became a cat guru," Mike said. People come to him with problems they're having with their kitties, and from experience he can sometimes help.

Mike likes how cats all have different personalities. "Every cat I've ever had in my life is just so different from the others, all having their own special quirks," he said. "I love how each one is unique. I love learning how each one wants to be loved."

Mike was raised with both cats and dogs. When he moved out on his own, he chose to have only cats. "I feel cats have more personality than dogs," he said. He has seldom been without a fur-friend and is partial to black and white cats. A cat from his childhood named Roxy, aka Fat Cat, was a tuxedo. He remembers Roxy as friendly. She liked to hang out and cuddle, and she always wanted to be close.

Mike and his wife, Asmara, have five cats. Four were adopted from Carol's Ferals in Grand Rapids, Michigan, and one was a barn kitten adopted from a friend. Three of them are tuxedo kitties. "It's a party at my place," Mike said.

The couple is planning to buy a house and start a family, but for now they're pet parents. Mike works in the warehouse at Gentex Corporation in Zeeland.

Four of their cats are named after Harry Potter characters: Draco, Luna, Albus and Charlie. Mike is a fan of the young wizard and has read all the books and watched the movies multiple times.

The cat with the non-conforming name is Finley—he had his name when the couple adopted him, and it seemed to fit him, so they kept it.

Mike frequently talks to his cats, and they often answer back. His standard reply is, "Really?" He suspects they're only asking for food. "They act like they're wasting away, but they're all kinda chunky," he admitted.

Let's meet the cats and learn about their quirks.

Albus is diabetic and is given insulin injections twice a day. A scratch on one of his eyes resulted in a recent visit to an ophthalmologist. The diabetes is a factor in the treatment, but his eye is slowly improving. Albus is a big love who makes biscuits and gives head bonks. He's the most chill of all the cats and is always sprawled out sleeping somewhere.

Charlie, the only orange cat, is a bit chunky and is a huge lover. He loves belly rubs and gentle smacks. His favorite toy is hair ties, so Asmara needs to hide them from him. "He loves my wife more than anyone and is always sleeping with her, whether on the couch or in bed," Mike said.

Finley is the resident house panther who acts like a dog. He's the first to approach anyone new to the house. He loves everyone, even if they aren't cat people. His favorite thing to do is lick people—weird. He loves to lay on Mike's lap while he plays video games.

Luna is the sassy lady of the house and runs the place. She chirps and meows when she hears her name. Her favorite toy was once a little hedgehog, but now it's just fabric and yarn—she loves to play fetch with it. "She'll bring it right back to you. She'll meow and paw at you until you throw it again," Mike explained.

Draco is the baby of the family and is the first cat they got as a couple. He has only-child syndrome. "He's the craziest of our cats. He loves to look at the birds and plot their demise while chattering at them," Mike said. Draco loves Mike more than anyone, except maybe Luna. Draco gets randomly scared and concerned about everyday objects, like hangers or cords. He will play with pretty much anything he can bat around and chase. One of the quirky things he does is groom Mike when he has facial hair.

"He's gotta make sure I'm clean enough for his standards," Mike joked.

The cats do seem to rule the house. Mike said the cats have more furniture than he and his wife do—there are six cat towers for them to climb and lounge on. Doors to the bedrooms and bathroom can't be closed. If they are, there's always a cat meowing "let me in."

The cats also rule in the bedroom. Albus's favorite spot to sleep is above Mike and Asmara's heads on their pillow. Luna will paw at their faces when they are trying to sleep and does so until they give her attention.

Having his own fur-family isn't enough for Mike. To quench his need to be around cats, he volunteers at rescues and has been doing so for more than seven years. For the first four years, he helped at Carol's Ferals in Grand Rapids, Michigan. When Carol's closed in 2021, disappointed volunteers formed Second Chance Cats of West Michigan. Mike has been helping at the new rescue for three years.

"I just like cats. It's an excuse to spend time with new ones," he said. Mike gives meds, sweeps floors, serves food, cleans litter boxes and interacts with the temporary residents. "That's the fun part," he said of holding, petting and playing with the cats.

He talks to them—sometimes in baby talk—while he performs his assigned chores. He tries to remember all their names. Newcomers are often scared and need to time to adjust—they swat or back away when he approaches. Mike said that each cat decides when the time is right to be petted; it can sometimes take months before he or she feels comfortable enough to be touched.

Mike has a soft spot for all the residents at Second Chance Cats. "It's bittersweet when they get adopted," he said. He often feels a tug at his heart to take a cat or two home, but knows the five he has at home comprises an already full house.

Cats aren't the only thing Mike loves. He also loves beer. In 2015, he started keeping track of how many different beers he has sampled. He's up to 1,367. When his two passions collided, Mike became a collector. He has close to 80 beer bottles and cans that either have a cat themed label or name.

One of his favorite brewers is Fat Orange Cat Brew Co. in Connecticut. The company uses bright colors and whimsical, cartoonish designs, including orange cats, on the beer cans. Some of their beers are named after cats such as Aquacat, All the Cool Cats on the Back of the Bus, Keep Yer Claws Sharp, Stay at Home Cat Dad and Baby Kittens.

Another favorite is 3 Gatos Brewery in Wyoming, Michigan. They have cat-themed beers such as Bengal, Maine Coon, American Bobtail and Cheshire.

One of his preferred beers is Psychedelic Cat Grass from Shorts Brewing Company in Bellaire, Michigan.

Mike also brews beer and gives his creations cat-themed names. He's made at least one beer after each of his cats: Tart Boy Draco Sour, Sassy Lady Luna Gose, Finney Cakes Porter, Chonka Chuck White Stout and Mr.

Albus Milk Stout. All his other beers have generic cat-related names which, he said, aren't as fun.

But Mike is definitely having fun. "I'm just like a crazy cat lady, but I'm a guy," he said.

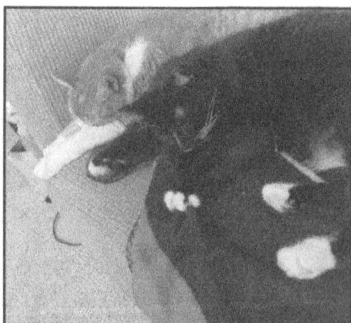

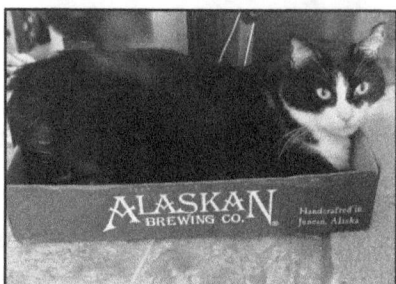

The Behrens' cats:
Top left: Luna
Top right: Albus and Charlie
Bottom left: Finley
Bottom right: Draco
(Photographs courtesy of Mike Behrens.)

After feeding time at Second Chance Cats of West Michigan, Mike Behrens spends time hanging out with the cats at the rescue. Pictured are Otis, Charley and Fred. *(Photograph by Janet Vormittag.)*

Below: Part of Mike Behrens' beer can collection. Each can has either a cat themed label or name. *(Photograph courtesy of Mike Behrens.)*

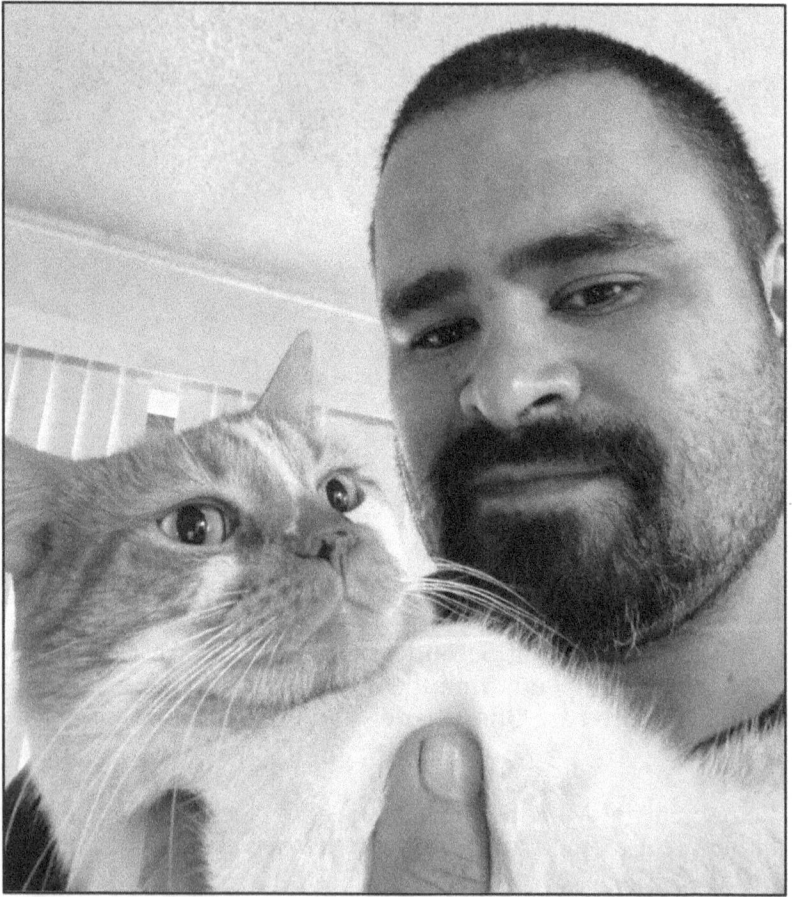

Joshua Ladd with Jinxie, a stray cat he helped get into a rescue. When the white and orange tabby didn't get adopted, Joshua adopted him. *(Photograph courtesy of Joshua Ladd.)*

Joshua Ladd

When Joshua Ladd and his wife, Sarah, divorced, they each took two of the four cats they had adopted as a couple. "I was upset, but it was the right thing to do," Joshua said.

It's been two years since his marriage ended, and Joshua is still emotional about the situation. "I don't miss the relationship, but I do miss the cats," he said. "They're always in my heart."

He added that the cats were the closest thing to children he would ever have. The feeling of leaving two cats behind was so raw he could hardly look at photos of his fur-babies on his phone.

When he was a kid, Joshua's family had dogs. He recalls only one cat, a dilute tortie named Kitty, but he wasn't into cats at the time.

When he met his wife-to-be, she had a long-haired calico named Libby. "That's when I became interested in cats," he said. Three and a half years later, Libby developed pancreatitis, resulting in euthanasia.

Missing Libby, the couple went to the Jackson Humane Society and adopted a tuxedo kitten named

Diesel. Two months later, they went back and adopted another kitten, a black polydactyl they named Vedder, after the lead singer in Pearl Jam.

When an white and orange tabby started hanging around outside the door to the apartment complex where Joshua and his wife lived, he took notice. Neighbors fed the stray, and it didn't take long for Joshua to start visiting with the friendly guy, which he named Jinxie.

"I didn't know if he was dumped or if he belonged to someone," Joshua said. After several months, he was able to get Jinxie into a rescue where he was neutered, vaccinated and put up for adoption. Joshua followed the cat's story on the rescue's Facebook page and was surprised and sad when no one wanted the friendly guy.

"We decided to adopt him," Joshua said. Jinxie and Joshua have a strong bond, developed, in part, when he cared for him as a stray. "I love them all, but he's my favorite cat."

Joshua gets upset and depressed about cats left behind or dumped or when their owners move. "I can't think about it," he said.

When Joshua's mother had a stray momma cat with kittens in her yard, he helped her neighbor catch the feline family. He wanted to keep a black kitten from the litter, but his wife said no. He was disappointed—to put it mildly.

To appease Joshua, the couple went to the humane society where they ended up adopting a cat named Hugs. They renamed him Atticus, but called him Attie.

"From day one, Attie chose me as his person—although I didn't really want him. It wasn't his fault. He was an innocent bystander," Joshua explained.

Attie is timid and skittish. "You have to be gentle with him," Joshua explained. "I'm blessed. I love him on his terms."

In the divorce, Joshua got Attie and Jinxie. His ex-wife took Diesel and Vedder—they had both been adopted in her name.

Having only two cats didn't last long for Joshua.

With winter approaching, his dad was worried about an outside cat he was feeding and asked his son if wanted the stray.

"I did," Joshua said. The black cat reminded him of Vedder, one of the cats his wife kept.

Joshua and his new girlfriend named the cat Milo, which means beloved. Milo was already neutered and had a microchip, but the owners couldn't be located.

"It was a big adjustment from living outside to living inside an apartment," Joshua said of bringing Milo home. At first, he kept the newcomer separated from Attie and Jinxie. When the three cats finally met, there was a lot of hissing, but it didn't take long for them to adjust to each another.

Milo had a hard time adapting to life inside—he had a strong desire to be outside. "He's sneaky, and I have to be careful," Joshua said.

Milo's persistence paid off when he slipped out the door early one morning as Joshua was leaving for work.

Joshua took a vacation day to search for the escapee. "It was worth it. I couldn't go to work with him outside."

Joshua spent hours walking in the subdivisions near his apartment complex looking for the missing Milo. After about five hours of searching, he spotted Milo in a brushy area. Using a can of wet food, he lured the run-away from his hiding spot. While Milo was savoring the meal, Joshua grabbed him. Milo wasn't happy, but Joshua was.

Joshua has a one-bedroom apartment, and guess who gets the bedroom? The cats. In the cats' room are comfy beds, litter boxes, a cat tree to climb and lots of toys.

Having their own bedroom doesn't stop the cats from sleeping with Joshua in the living room. Jinx developed a habit of pawing his human in the middle of night until he wakes. "He wants food," Joshua explained. When it first happened, he made the mistake of getting up and giving the persistent beggar a snack. Now it's a nightly routine, sometimes it happens more than once a night.

Jinx even taught Milo the trick. "They act like they never eat," Joshua said. He added that it was annoying, and he should break them of the habit, but admitted having cats is worth interrupted sleep.

"I'm at the mercy of the cats," he joked.

Joshua's passion for cats shows in his home's décor. He has wall hangings and pillows with cat sayings such as, *Rescue is my favorite breed; Time spent with a cat is never wasted; You had me at meow; My shelter cat rescued me.*

He has more than a thousand photos on his phone, the majority of which are his cats. They're always doing something cute worthy of a photo. "I'm a little obsessed with cats," Joshua admitted.

When his grandmother passed away the previous year, his dad asked Joshua if he wanted her framed cat pictures. Of course he did. The artwork now decorates the walls in the cats' room. Joshua said his grandma wasn't a cat person, and he has no idea why she had the pictures, but he appreciates them.

What does Joshua like about cats? He likes their independence and attitude—a cat's affection is hard to win. He loves their meows and "biscuit making" when they knead with their paws. He loves the feel of their tongues when they give a kiss and the sound of their purrs when they're happy.

"I love dogs, but I love cats more—barking drives me crazy," he said.

Joshua is especially attracted to adult cats, even special-needs cats. "The ones nobody wants," he explained. He would love to start a cat rescue, and maybe he will when he has his own house with more space.

"I'm very passionate about animals. I want to save them all."

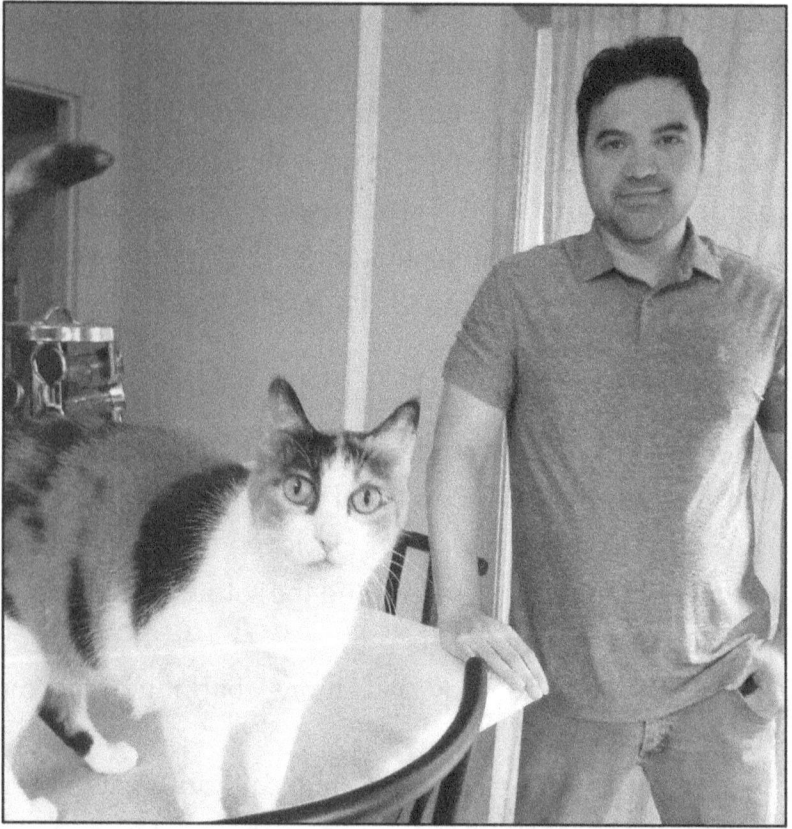

Arvin Candelaria and Mirra who was found in the engine compartment of a car towed from Detroit to Muskegon. Below are two of the cats who have traveled to several states with Arvin and his family. Left is DJ, short for Dumpling Jr. and D2, a Dumpling look-alike. *(Photographs courtesy of Arvin Candelaria.)*

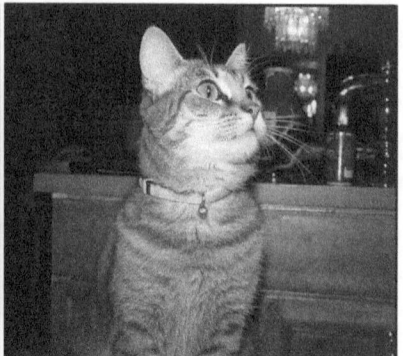

Arvin Candelaria

When Arvin Candelaria was growing up, his family often moved. Cats were one of the steadfast factors in his life. "Our friends were our cats," he said.

Arvin was born in the Philippines, and for the first nine years of his life, he lived with his grandparents. He had been given a kitten when he was young—perhaps two or three years old, he's not sure of the exact age. The family had several cats, but Princess, a gray tiger, belonged to him. Arvin has been partial to gray tabbies ever since.

Arvin's mom, a United States citizen, studied pre-med in the Philippines. She joined the army in 1990 and was stationed at Fort Gordon in Augusta, Georgia, in 1993. When Arvin was nine, his mom flew him and his brother and sister to join her in the States. Arvin had to leave Princess behind. "My grandparents kept her," he said. Whenever he talked to them, he asked about his cat.

In Augusta, Arvin's family lived in a trailer park. "There were cats that everyone took care of," Arvin recalled. Two in particular hung around their trailer: a young white female they named Puti (which means "white" in the Filipino language) and the other one, an old tomcat, they named Dumpling. There was also a Dumpling look-alike they named DJ—short for Dumpling Jr.

None of the cats were fixed. When Puti was expecting a litter, she found a private place to give birth somewhere in the underside of the family's trailer. "We could hear the kittens meowing, so we investigated," Arvin said. "We had to cut through the mesh underneath the trailer to get them."

They brought the mom-cat and her three kittens inside and named the little ones Snowball, Squeaks and D2 respectively. D2 looked like Dumpling, the park cat suspected of being his dad.

"D2 was similar to Princess, so I decided he was my cat," Arvin said.

Three years after moving to Augusta, his mom left the military to do her medical residency at a hospital in Macon and relocated the trailer to a park in the new city. Included in the trip were five cats: Puti, Snowball, Squeaks, D2 and DJ. The elderly Dumpling had died before the move.

"We're a cat family," Arvin said. It was unthinkable to leave them behind.

The family stayed in Macon for three years. Unfortunately, Puti got hit by a car and didn't survive. The new trailer park didn't have a shortage of strays though, and when two started to hang around their trailer, the family named them Windstar and Stripe.

"Basically, we adopted strays," Arvin said. Eventually, they spayed/neutered all the cats.

In 1999, the family moved to New York, allowing Arvin's mom to finish her last year of residency at a hospital in the Bronx. They drove from Macon to New York with all six cats—D2, DJ, Squeaks, Snowball, Windstar and Stripe—and a stray Pomeranian they had taken in and named Chip. They rented a house in White Plains, New York, and from this point on, the cats stayed indoors.

After his mom finished her residency in New York, she reenlisted in the Army as an officer. She was to be stationed in Alaska, but had to do her training in Texas first, so the family drove to Texas with six cats and one dog. Arvin began his sophomore year in San Antonio, and in November they packed up, fur-family included, and flew to Fairbanks, Alaska, where Arvin finished the rest of high school.

In the summer of 2003, Arvin's mom left the Army once more. "She took a job at Hackley Hospital in Muskegon, Michigan, so we flew from Alaska to Michigan with all six cats and one dog still with us," he said. "We kept those cats the whole time."

Arvin attended Muskegon Community College until he joined the U.S. Air Force in 2006. Whenever he called home, he asked about the cats, and when he was on leave, he visited them.

Arvin was stationed in Okinawa, Japan, and his first deployment was to Iraq. A second deployment took him to the United Arab Emirates (UAE). His second station was Minot, North Dakota, which is where he met a woman, Velvet Lyght. When he was discharged from the Air Force, the couple decided to move to Muskegon.

While Arvin was in the military, his sister, Iris (also a cat lover), took all six cats with her when she went to the University of Michigan in Ann Arbor. Years later, when she returned to Muskegon, she brought back 18-year-old Snowball, the only cat still living.

Arvin went to Baker College, earning a degree in digital media design, and now works as a freelance videographer. Velvet found a job as shelter manager at Big Lake Humane Society in Muskegon, where Arvin volunteers. He looks after the cats when they attend special events. He also offers his videography skills for promotional materials.

"I always stop by the cat room whenever I visit the shelter," he said.

Keeping up with family tradition, Arvin and Velvet's first cat was a stray. "A friend found her in his car engine," Arvin explained. The car had just been towed from Detroit—the friend had no idea where or when or how the cat took refuge in the vehicle. The friend jokingly called the stowaway Greaser. Arvin and Velvet changed her name to Mirra.

Mirra was an inside cat. One day, however, a neighborhood kid left their door open, and the inquisitive cat decided to investigate the great outdoors. Arvin guessed she was trying to find a way back into the house when she crawled under the porch and became stuck behind a beam. "We had to use a chainsaw to cut her out," Arvin said. After that, Mirra was content being a house cat.

While Arvin has always taken in strays, he has one adopted cat. Velvet recognized the gray-tiger theme in Arvin's life, and when Fossil, an older friendly gray tabby, came into the humane society, she brought him home as a surprise for Arvin. Fossil passed away of old age a few years ago.

The stray cat theme continues: Velvet befriended a stray who then took up residence on their porch. They dubbed her "Porch Cat," but the friendly kitty comes in the house whenever she wants.

One of things Arvin particularly likes about cats is their purr. "It's soothing. They're relaxed. It matches my temperament." He also likes that they're easy to care for and fairly self-sufficient.

The couple also have two dogs now, and Arvin is fine with dogs, but cats are number one in his life. "If I have to choose between dogs and cats, I'll always choose cats."

Scott Harris and Tasha, a goofy, loyal and loving feline companion. *(Photograph courtesy of Scott Harris.)*

Scott Harris

When asked if he had any photos of himself with cats, Scott Harris searched his Apple Photo App, which resulted in 170 pictures. "Is that enough?" he asked.

Scott has a unique relationship with cats. "We don't own cats. We cohabitate with them. I cohabitate with seven," he said.

Scott's awareness of cats started as a kid. A neighbor had free-range cats, and his dad disapproved. Scott learned there were two teams when it came to pets: Team Dog and Team Cat. An independent thinker, Scott came up with his own team: Team why?

Fast forward to college. Scott's girlfriend wanted a cat, so they went to the Ingham County Humane Society in Lansing, Michigan, and adopted a gray cat named Kayla. Then the girlfriend found a kitten and brought it to Scott's apartment. The kitten, named Philip, bonded with Kayla. "A year later she [the girlfriend] decided she didn't want a boyfriend, and she didn't want any cats," Scott said. So, Scott was left alone with Kayla and Philip.

"That was the beginning of my love and respect for cats," he said. The kitties helped him survive being alone, and he considered them his friends.

Scott has a tattoo of Kayla on his upper arm, which, he explained, in the tribe of people who like both cats and tattoos, it's called a *cattoo*.

The most cats Scott has ever had at one time is 15. That was with his late wife, Debbie. They all had been rescues or adopted from the Ingham County Animal Shelter where Scott volunteered and served on the Board of Directors.

Debbie had a cat when Scott met her—it was a sign, surely. On the couple's first date, they rescued a kitten who had climbed too high in a tree. Deb's neighbor took in the wayward climber.

Two years after meeting, Debbie and Scott married, and their love of cats was evident at their wedding. Instead of the traditional groom and bride atop the wedding cake, they had four ceramic cats representing their own cats. Scott said having cats as a cake topper was a mutual idea. To seal their obsession, they wore almost-matching T-shirts as they left the wedding. Scott's said *Daddy Kitty* and Deb's said *Mama Kitty*.

When Debbie was expecting their first child, Scott had a special maternity shirt created for her—*Kitten on Board* was printed on it.

When asked if they had a name selected for their firstborn. Scott would jokingly say, "Smokey or Pumpkin." Scott believes in giving cats human names. He began to realize the importance of names when, in high school, he was going to name a cat Airhead. Someone pointed out that it wasn't a very kind name. Instead, he chose Princess. "We're all evolving. We're all learning," he said, adding that names can become a self-fulfilling prophecy. By applying a label, it can affect the perception of the cat. Name the cat Airhead, and she will be—or perceived to be—an airhead. By the way, Debbie and Scott did *not* give their two children cat names.

Tragically, in 2002, 15 years after their wedding, Debbie died from a chronic heart condition leaving Scott alone to raise 8-year-old Maddie and 4-year-old Sawyer.

One of the couple's dreams was to open a bookstore, and Scott was adamant that dream would still come true. In 2006, he opened *Everybody Reads, Books and Stuff* in Lansing. Maddie designed the store's logo, which included the face of a cat.

Three months after the store opened, on a nasty autumn day, meows were heard outside the backdoor. When Scott opened the door, a skinny wet kitten walked in as if she belonged there. She soon found a warm place to rest—on Scott's shoulder. She trusted him. Felt comfortable with him. He read her actions as, "You and I were meant to be together."

Although for the rest of her life she would be called, "Kitten," he named the newcomer Reed, and, as it turned out, she wasn't a kitten, but a malnourished young cat. Scott took her home.

"She was the first cat that I recognized expressing gratitude," Scott said. "It was so visible."

Reed sat on his lap and stared at him. She always wanted to be near him. "I promised her if she ever becomes human, I'd marry her," he said. So far, she has decided to remain a cat.

Scott admits the promise was problematic when he dated. He is now gratefully engaged to an understanding woman with two of her own cats. He met Tams Nicholson on a Facebook group for Vegan Singles over 50.

"Tams not only cohabited with cats, but her recognition that cats are fellow sentients and not property, jibed so very well with my beliefs, an attribute that I found—and still find—very attractive," Scott explained.

Not only cats have Scott's respect. He's been involved in the animal rights movement since the 1970s. He was the president of the Michigan Federation of Humane Societies and Animal Advocates for three years. Scott finds that all species can teach us, if we're open to learning.

Tams shares his passion for animals. She is the executive director of All-Creatures.org.

Scott said he learned a lot about cats from reading *All Cats have Asperger Syndrome*, the early version of *All Cats are on the Autism Spectrum*. For example, too much stimulation, especially noises, can be overwhelming to humans on the autistic spectrum. The same thing can overwhelm cats.

Scott said cats can teach us so much, that we just have to pay attention. Things he has learned from his cats include patience, unconditional love, the importance of being in the moment and the importance of play.

"I find comfort in the companionship of felines. It's a legitimate friendship. The relationship is just as powerful as with a human." He added that the relationship is symbiotic. "They accept us with all our flaws."

Scott Harris and Kitten, aka Reed. Kitten passed on 8/25/24.

Scott's tribute to Kitten on Facebook: Maybe a dozen years ago I attended a Michigan Humane Society Lobby Day at the Michigan Capitol. One of the speakers shared that living with a companion animal affords us an opportunity to become friends with another species. Anyone who has experienced the unconditional joyful love from a companion animal understands just how simple, profound and true this is. Today, I lost one of my closest friends. Kitten (aka, "Reed") and I met on a rainy September evening in 2008. I was working at the bookstore and when I glanced out at the parking lot. I noticed a kitten dodging the raindrops. I opened the back door to the store and Kitten walked right in. Within a couple of days, she would jump up onto my desk, wrap herself on my shoulders and fall asleep. Not only was I smitten, it wasn't long before I started telling people that if ever she became human, she and I would marry. She never became human and I never became feline, but today she became an angel. The deep sadness will eventually abate. The gratitude to our Creator for allowing Kitten and me to share time on earth is eternal. Thank you Kitten for being my friend. You are loved, missed and appreciated. *(Photograph courtesy of Scott Harris.)*

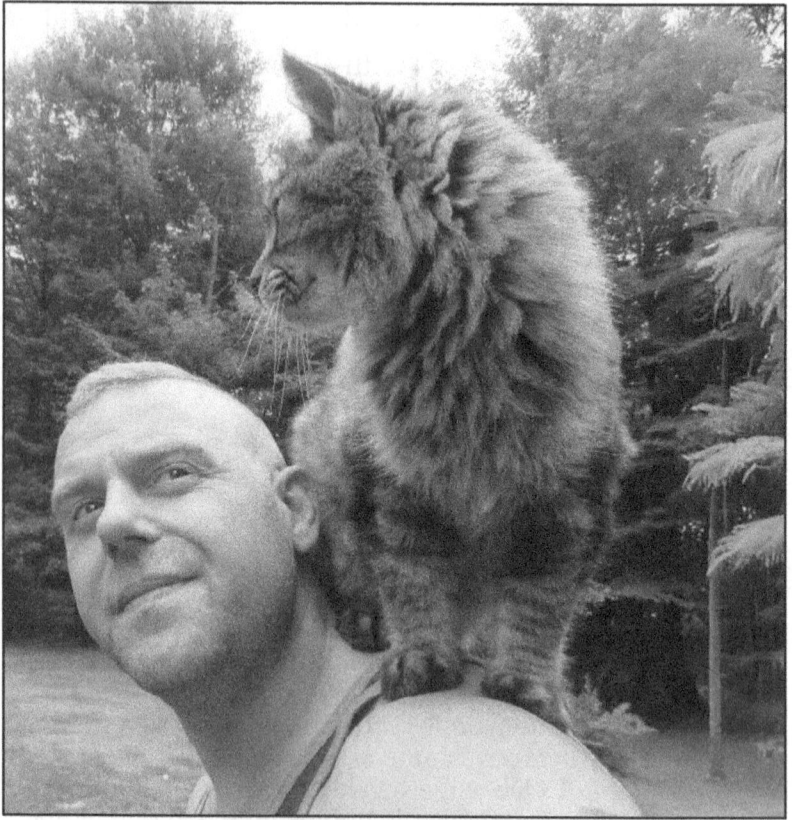

Eric Langland with Pickle, one of the cats he rescued on the day the sick kitty was scheduled to be euthanized. Pickle became Eric's best pal. Below: Eric with Snally, a cuddly outdoor cat. (*Photographs courtesy of Eric Langland.*)

Eric Langland

Eric Langland was born a cat person. "My family had a sweet gray kitty named Punky, who I remember either watching over me from the dresser top or sleeping in bed with me," he recalls.

As a kid, Eric had several pets—cats, dogs, guinea pigs, birds, fish and whatever other animals he rescued. He remembers his first litter of kittens were white with blue eyes. Growing up, he was always rescuing something, but mostly cats, which was severely frowned upon by his dad. "Dad always hated me bringing animals home, but my mom was fine with it," he said. "Dad didn't seem to understand or appreciate my merciful disposition towards animals. He was a hunter and had more enjoyment from killing animals and eating them than from helping them and appreciating their existence."

His Dad's outlook on animals didn't stop Eric from rescuing animals, nor did it change his philosophy. "Animals are more like humans than most people know, and we behave more like animals than most humans will admit," he said.

Eric recalls the times without cats as being lonely and sad.

Mr. Pickle Pants (aka Tiger) and Mini Moose were two special cats in Eric's life. Several years ago, Eric adopted the two least adoptable cats from the county humane society—a semi-feral momma and a sick little guy, who was going to be euthanized that day. Pickle knew he had been saved and became Eric's best pal.

"We adopted him not long before I became disabled. I would not be here without that cat. He was always there and seemed to know what I was going through, like a little angel," Eric said.

Eric has a variety of medical issues. In 1999, when he was in high school, an accident caused severe head and spine injuries. Then in 2008, he came down with an extreme case of fibromyalgia and was prescribed sedatives. The drugs caused him to fall, which resulted in permanent injuries. He eventually quit the prescriptions and switched to vitamins and supplements.

Eric never thought about volunteering until he went with his mother to an animal shelter and overheard staff talking about volunteers. He asked if people could work with only cats. After he became disabled, he started volunteering at Harbor Humane Society in Ottawa County, Michigan, and BestPals Animal Rescue in Holland, Michigan.

For nearly ten years, Eric gave his time and energy to helping cats. He cleaned kennels, took the time to learn each cat's personality and wrote their adoption profiles.

Because he knew each cat's temperament, he could help people find the perfect kitty to fit their lifestyle. Eric often stepped forward on holidays when other volunteers were with their families. He also helped with orientation of new volunteers.

Eric has fostered hundreds of cats—he lost count but estimates the number to be between 500 and 600. He said his experience working as a certified nursing assistant, sometimes in psych units, was one reason he fostered sick, injured or insane kitties. His work with fearful, aggressive and feral cats helped make them adoptable.

"It was either I fostered them, or they would've been euthanized. The babies and most of the moms turned out amazing and adoptable." He still has one mom-cat who stayed skittish for a long time but loves to be petted now—but only in her snuggle box. She prefers to live in the garage with her friends, and she keeps the vehicles free of mice.

"You never know what will happen. I've had the most feral cats ever turn into total marshmallow indoor kitties."

Once, about 10 years ago, Eric was caring for 30 fosters, including feral moms and their kittens, when he had six of his own indoor and three outdoor cats to take care of at the same time. Eric is good at keeping the unadoptable and stray cats.

Baby is a large Maine Coon mix who showed up with his brother ten years ago. Eric managed to make friends with him after a couple of months and after receiving a few good bites. Baby was sick and injured, so Eric patched him up and had him neutered. "He has many scars and injuries from his super feral days," Eric said. Baby hates being indoors, unless it's in the garage in wintertime. He does love to be petted and held though.

Little Dude showed up last year—Eric thinks a neighbor TNR'd (trap-neuter-return) the young cat, but Little Dude decided to call Eric's garage home. Eric is trying to get him to live indoors but so far Little Dude isn't interested. The black and white cat loves to be held and is one of the gentlest cats Eric has ever met.

Snally was found outside and nearly dead by the time Eric got him home. He worked his medical magic, and the gray cat came back to life. Snally is mostly an outdoor kitty but comes in when it's super cold. He loves being outside with his adopted dad, The Grafton Monster. "They follow me around the yard like a little gang," Eric said. Snally is super cuddly, unless he thinks you're going to clean his ears or give him meds, then he's paranoid.

Eric has been a gardener for over 30 years and said gardens are boring without some goofball cat helping pull weeds. He also has a graveyard in the woods that's quite lovely in the spring, due to all the flowers around the gravestones.

Nowadays, pain makes it hard for Eric to even get out of the house, which he said is fine, since some of his cats require more care. Eric has about a half dozen indoor cats who are old, disabled or have been traumatized by humans. He cleans litter boxes two times a day, which helps keep him in shape. He also cares for a few outdoor semi-feral cats. People dump cats where he lives, and his ferals bring the newcomers to his home for food or medical attention. He said cats recognize that he cares about them—even the wild ones will be friendly at times.

"I suffer every second of every day, but knowing what these creatures go through instilled a drive to help the suffering, or at least help them pass as peacefully as possible," he explained.

Eric's wife, Kristine, is fine with his rescuing animals, and his mom helps with food and sometimes medical bills. Kristine's best buddy is Mr. Chubby Cheeks, an ex-feral who destroyed a vet's office, so Eric was asked to take the wildcat. "He gave me a few decent bites but was a super easy rehab after being neutered," Eric said.

Eric finds all cats adorable with unique personalities but sees them as the underdogs in life. "Guess I have a similar personality to them, and I will never make the claim of being sane from the human point of view."

Bill Hoffmann with Romeo, a stray cat who brought him back to life after a series of life-altering events. Top: Romeo at a work site. *(Photographs courtesy of Bill Hoffmann.)*

Bill Hoffmann Jr

Bill Hoffmann's job loss had a cascading effect: He lived on savings until they were gone. He lost his house. He got divorced. Depression set in. He was homeless for three months and had to live with a friend.

A stray cat he named Romeo brought him back to life. "He helped me learn about myself. I was very much a control person, and he taught me to let go," Bill explained.

Bill used to put out food for neighborhood critters, including stray cats. He first noticed Romeo when he was just a kitten joining the other critters to eat. The black cat grew up to be a bully who fought with other hungry strays. Bill didn't know how to deal with the aggression.

Bill turned to Michelle Kenat, a friend from the theater, for advice. Michelle, a pet advocate, suggested he live-trap the cat and have him neutered. At the time, Bill was directing *Romeo and Juliet* at the Holland Civic Theater and named the stray after the ill-fated lover.

"I decided to trap him after he showed signs of trauma and extreme fear of people," Bill explained. Romeo was about two years old at the time. Bill kept

Romeo inside for months after the surgery, but befriending the feisty cat seemed impossible.

"He was yearning to be outside," Bill recalled. "Against my better judgement, I let him go free with a collar and ID." To his surprise, Romeo returned. They settled into a routine: Bill let Romeo out in the evening, and the weary prowler returned in the morning and slept away the day on Bill's bed. A year later, Romeo tested positive for FIV (feline immunodeficiency virus). Bill decided his friend's free-roaming days were over, and the three-year-old was no longer allowed outside, except on a leash.

Meanwhile, Bill reinvented himself. His days of being an automotive engineer were long gone. His new occupation was that of a self-employed handyman.

He helped his friend Michelle convert two rooms of her home into a haven for fosters—one for isolation and the other for free-roaming cats. Michelle worked at Harbor Humane Society. At that time, close to 30 cats were euthanized each week at the shelter. To save more animals, Michelle started BestPals Animal Rescue Center in Holland, Michigan, and bought a bigger house with space for the nonprofit rescue. Bill used his handyman skills to help Michelle's team transform an outbuilding into a shelter for adoptable animals, until homes could be found for them.

Over the years, Harbor Humane transitioned to a no-kill facility, which inspired Bill to become involved. His self-employment as a handyman afforded him flexible hours. He also became a transport driver, shuttling dogs to groomers, and transporting both cats and dogs to shelters with open kennel space.

His most memorable drive was to Michigan's Upper Peninsula, which he thought was a six-hour drive. He loaded nine cats and two dogs into the shelter's van at 9 a.m. and hit the road. After he crossed the Mackinac Bridge, he realized that Copper Harbor Humane Society was in Houghton, in the Keweenaw Peninsular. The drive time was double what he had expected—he didn't arrive until 10:30 p.m. After unloading his precious cargo, he headed home. About midnight, he reached Marquette and realized he was too tired to continue driving. He found a place to park and slept in the van for a few hours before completing the journey.

Romeo sometimes joined Bill at work. At first, Romeo didn't enjoy riding in the truck—he'd hunker down on the floor and howl. But he caught on fast. "He was one of the smartest cats," Bill said.

Bill recalls Romeo keeping him company while stripping the exterior paint off a house and garage and at various landscaping jobs. He also took Romeo along while he built theater sets for West Michigan Savoyards and Holland Civic Theatre.

In 2022, when he was around 14 years old, Romeo became sick and couldn't be saved. "It rips me up to think on it," Bill said. He is adamant that people should be with their cat or dog when they pass. "You need to be there when they die. It's not easy, but it's your duty."

Bill had Romeo's collar made into a bracelet, with the purple heart-shaped ID tag still attached. To this day, he wears the remembrance bracelet, taking it off only for medical procedures.

Looking back over the pets in his life, Bill realizes that he wasn't always the ideal pet parent.

When he married, the couple had a "fancy" house, so they had their cats declawed to prevent them from doing damage to the furniture or woodwork. "I would never declaw again," he said. He compared declawing to cutting off fingertips. In observing cats, he's realized the importance of claws. He now regularly clips his cats' nails. Bill recommends looking at things from a cat's point of view. Would you want your nails removed?

Bill said he owes a lot to Romeo and Michelle regarding his education on understanding animals. "I don't think of them as disposable. They're family for life."

Sometimes Bill wears a T-shirt with a black tabby cat on it that reads, *I would push you in front of zombies to save my cat.* He wears it mostly to large public gatherings, such as the Michigan Renaissance Festival. "I get lots of nods, smiles, thumbs up and comments from folks. It's definitely a conversation starter," he said.

Bill continues to help Michelle with her rescue, including when people call about a cat stuck in a tree. If he can reach the cat with his 22-foot ladder, he makes the climb. Smelly sardines are his go-to food to entice a cat on a limb to come to him. If the cat is too high, he'll call in a tree trimmer or other expert at scaling trees.

Bill now has two cats: Vahla and Gwenny. He recommends fostering-to-adopt to see if a cat is a good fit. If possible, go to a rescue and sit with the cats. "Let the cat choose you," he said. "All cats have their own personalities. It's amazing how different and unique and special they are."

He also recommends volunteering for a rescue. "It's worth it—for you and the animals. It's so gratifying," he said. "I'm hoping someone reads this story, not only to learn that cats are great companions, but to realize they need our help."

Bill Hoffmann hanging out with a mom-cat and her kittens at BestPals Animal Rescue. (*Photograph by Janet Vormittag.*)

About the Author

Janet Vormittag is an animal advocate, author and friend to any stray cat in her neighborhood. Since 2006, she has published *Cats and Dogs, a Magazine Devoted to Companion Animals* which is a free local magazine. She has written three novels and three non-fiction cat-themed books. Janet has a degree in journalism from Grand Valley State University and was a correspondent for The Grand Rapids Press for ten years. She enjoys hiking, vegan fare, flower gardening, kayaking, movies, exploring her home state and reading. Janet and her cats live in West Michigan. www.janetvormittag.com

Advance Praise

"*Jerry's Vegan Women* takes you on a roller coaster ride of emotions, from laughter and excitement to disdain and heartbreak for what might have been. It's an irreverent and fun look at the intersection of dietary and relationship ethics. You won't want to put it down."

> — Paul Shapiro, Vice President of Farm Animal Protection, The Humane Society of the United States

"*Jerry's Vegan Women* is an absorbing collection of stories about a thoughtful guy whose life is changed through his relationships with vegan women. Through Shaberman's storytelling, the reader empathizes with Jerry and his compassion for our planet's amazing animal kingdom."

> — Carole Hamlin, Board Member, Vegetarian Resource Group

"You don't have to be hardcore vegan to enjoy and appreciate the engaging — and often insightful — stories of Ben Shaberman. He writes with flair, humor, and compassion about characters, relationships, and situations that have a universal appeal, even to the steak-and-potatoes reader."

> — Roland Goity, Editor, *WIPs: Works (of Fiction) in Progress Literary Journal*

"The most engaging aspect of Ben Shaberman's writing is his distinctive voice. Typically lighthearted, often amusing, Ben's voice grabs you by the hand and pulls you along for an entertaining ride."

> — Tiffany Hauck, Editor, *Split Infinitive Literary Journal*